GOD WAITS

Faith from the Back Pew

Lois Flores

make life colorful

Portland, Oregon

Copyright © 2023 by Lois Flores
All rights reserved.

No part of this publication may be reproduced, distributed, or transmitted in any form or by any means, including photocopying, recording, or other electronic or mechanical methods, without the prior written permission of the publisher or author, except as permitted by U.S. copyright law. For permission requests, please contact Lois@LoisFlores.com

ISBN 979-8-9880220-0-8

This book is a memoir. It reflects the author's present recollections of her experiences, as she perceived them. Some events have been compressed, and some dialogue has been re-created.

Scripture quotations marked (NIV) are taken from the Holy Bible, New International Version®, NIV®. Copyright © 1973, 1978, 1984, 2011 by Biblica, Inc.™ Used by permission of Zondervan. All rights reserved worldwide. www.zondervan.com. The "NIV" and "New International Version" are trademarks registered in the United States Patent and Trademark Office by Biblica, Inc.™

Cover Design © 2023 by Lois Flores
Cover Production © 2023 by Tay Juncker, j designs
Art by Kimmie Olson: @warriorofgrace on Instagram
Editor: Ann Sargent

First printing, 2023

Published by Red Tennies
www.RedTennies.com

*I dedicate my words to God, who gave them to me.
May they encourage you.*

CONTENTS

Introduction
I'M GLAD YOU'RE HERE   1

Section One
THE UNCERTAINTY OF FAITH   7

WHO I WAS   9

Chapter 1
MORE THAN A PRODIGAL DAUGHTER   11

Chapter 2
PITCHBACKS AND SLIP 'N SLIDES   17

Chapter 3
CHURCH KID   33

Chapter 4
SOMETHING IS MISSING   47

Chapter 5
WELCOME HOME   63

Section Two
THE PERFECT JOB FOR AN IMPERFECT PERSON   85

WHO I BECAME   87

Chapter 6
WOULD YOU LIKE TO WORK HERE?   89

Chapter 7
DOES GOD ATTEND STAFF MEETINGS?   95

Chapter 8
DO I HAVE TO GO TO CHURCH?   115

Chapter 9
WHAT'S IT GOING TO TAKE?   131

Chapter 10
WHY DOES THIS HURT SO MUCH?   141

Chapter 11
WOULD I DO THIS AGAIN?   159

Section Three
SPIRITUALLY UNDISCIPLINED   161

WHO I THOUGHT I WAS   163

Chapter 12
THE SILENT AMEN   165

Chapter 13
GATHERING DUST   179

Chapter 14
PULL UP A CHAIR   191

Chapter 15
UNWRITTEN WORDS   203

Section Four
LESSONS LEARNED AND LEARNING   215

WHO I REALLY AM   217

Chapter 16
TRUST ISSUES   219

Chapter 17
I WANT TO GO TO CHURCH   235

Chapter 18
LETTING LOVE IN   247

Chapter 19
ANYTHING CAN HAPPEN   267

Chapter 20
WELL DONE   279

Chapter 21
FOREVER GRATEFUL   289

Resources for You   303

REFLECTIONS ABOUT LABELS   305

MUSIC AND MENTIONS   309

PEOPLE WHO INSPIRE ME   313

A FEW BOOKS I FOUND HELPFUL   315

Introduction
I'M GLAD YOU'RE HERE

ON SUNDAYS, I WOULD LOOK at the people sitting in the pews of the church building and ask myself, "Why is everybody else a better Christian?" I would gaze across this sea of believers, and frequently compared my reserved demeanor to the outward displays of those around me. I assumed my faith wasn't as solid as the faith of those who would raise their hands during worship songs or kneel on the floor during prayers. I had convinced myself I wasn't a good enough Christian because I didn't talk about God or tell people Jesus was my best friend.

I had a past that wouldn't allow me the freedom to believe God accepted and loved me completely. I grew up believing I had to do things the right way to be valuable. I questioned if my faith was genuine, or merely inherited from my parents, and I even walked away from church.

I no longer believe I'm the only one who has struggled with doubt or feels like a "lesser than" Christian. I don't think I'm the only one who doesn't want to go to church every Sunday. I know I'm not the only one who doesn't read the Bible, pray regularly, or journal.

If you can relate to this, I want you to know you are not alone in feeling this way. I give you permission to admit it. It's time to quit comparing our faith to what we see around us. No more judging ourselves, we're terrible at it. I want you to find a relationship with God, not simply attend a local church.

Hope. Encouragement. This is what I want for you. There is strength in numbers. There is comfort in being included. We often shame ourselves for not being perfect Christians. We spend so much time trying to be good churchgoers, we forget we are children of God, all the while thinking we are the only one floundering.

God loves us and waits for us to figure that out. Our life is full when we live it on God's terms instead. It's time to stop defining Christianity as a checklist of obligations and start living as God's unconditionally loved children.

When I thought I was a failure as a Christian, I felt certain I was alone in that. I thought I was weak. I believed it was up to me to figure it out by myself. I feared it was too late. I was wrong. If any of this resonates with you, let me encourage you to be diligent in perseverance.

Please do not allow anybody to judge your faith journey—ever. That includes you. We can sometimes be the worst critics and judges as we compare our faith to what we think we see in others, or what we expect of ourselves. God is the only one who truly knows our heart and what each unique walk will look like. Let's trust Him with our faith, together. I thought I was always running away from one thing or toward another. Now I wonder if maybe, just maybe, I was running to **someone** instead. I love the Philips, Craig, and Dean song, "When God Ran," because it conveys the beautiful image of God coming to greet us.

When I began writing this book, I was on staff at the church I was attending. You will discover that story woven throughout these pages because it played an important role in my journey of faith. There were countless highs and lows in those nineteen years that it was my church home. Life was like one of those giant bungee cord rides that catapults you into the sky one moment then drops you over a cliff on the rebound where you are certain you see death staring you in the face, and secretly you sometimes hoped the band would snap.

You'll discover that this book isn't about church, nor about a church job. It is a book about an ordinary person who was in all the right places and given all the religious background and information, and still walked away from faith. This is about a spiritual struggle that is far more common than you can imagine. However, it is a story of discovery and victory.

I am not giving you the inside scoop about one congregation; I am here to share the influence working there had on my spiritual walk and why I think my story can help encourage others. You likely did not work at a church, but there are obstacles that can trip us up no matter where our daily routine takes us. If you have imagined what "church work" might look like, I may burst that idea bubble. As you read about some of my experiences working there, you may feel disheartened. Like a young woman exchanging her tiny hometown for the bright lights of the big city, I had my own expectations of what it would be like to be a church employee. Let's just say reality did not exceed those expectations. However, I was the perfect person for one of the most imperfect jobs out there. I was also the most imperfect person for one of the most perfect jobs in the world.

I was a volunteer or an employee for all but one of the years I was at that church. You will read about some of my frustrations with church work. Some fantastic things happened also, but this book is about my faith journey and those moments weren't the rocks that made it a bumpy road. Please understand and remember that my purpose in sharing these stories is to encourage you to persevere.

I am still connected to my previous congregation and continue to lead an outreach ministry there. I deeply love the people and I respect the leadership. We have all grown along this journey of faith and made many wonderful memories together. I deliberately chose not to name the church because I only wish the very best for them and I don't want to risk anybody thinking poorly of them. They are a precious group of people serving God diligently.

I was in what many would consider the perfect job in a seemingly easy place to remain strong in my faith and grow deeper in my relationship with God. I want you to know that it is never about your surroundings. It is about you. Yes, your surroundings will have an influence, but don't lose yourself within them. Never settle for anything less than what God has designed for you and placed on your heart. Please don't let anybody tell you what faith looks like for you. Nobody gets to use the word "should" when they are describing another person—they don't get to set the standards for your faith. Please do not allow anybody, or yourself, to judge your faith journey . . . ever. God is the only one who truly knows your heart and what your unique walk will look like.

At one time, I made a blanket assumption that all churches were the same once you peeked behind the scenes. I am thankful this isn't accurate, or I may not have returned to church. While the details in this book are true of my personal experiences and those of many around me who shared their stories along the way, they are not true of all churches. I am not working at my new church, and I couldn't tell you with certainty if I would choose to if the opportunity presented itself. I am wounded. I am weary. I am burned out. I am possibly a lot like you.

However, I'm here to share my story with the hope that as you identify with pieces of it, you will feel encouraged to keep going. I lost sight of God even though I grew up with church, attended a Christian college, and worked at a church. Eventually, I found Him in a deeper and far more meaningful way than I ever would have if I hadn't walked away. Spoiler alert. It's not about church, it's about love.

Section One

The Uncertainty of Faith

Who I Was

God, you waited for me to come to you, while knowing You would wait again for me to return. You watched me wander through life as I questioned my faith and tried to fill the emptiness. You waited for me to understand it was You who was missing in my life.

Thank you for waiting.

Chapter 1

MORE THAN A PRODIGAL DAUGHTER

"MY GREATEST CONCERN IS THIS. Have you turned your back on Jesus?"

A dear friend of mine asked me that in 1992. I wasn't going to church at the time, so it was a valid inquiry. But it stung. If I could have peered into a rearview mirror, I would have seen the line I said I would never cross. As I answered his question, I realized I had strayed so far from God, that, for the first time, I wasn't sure I could return. I had spent five years wandering in a spiritual desert, refusing to decide about pursuing my faith. I kept a small part of myself in the search, believing it counted for something with God, but honestly, I had quit seeking answers.

I had everything going for me in the faith department. I grew up in a Christian family, I attended church diligently through childhood, and I even attended a Christian college. Later, I worked in a church. None of that prevented my spiritual unrest.

I walked away from the church, and God, as a young adult. Even after returning to a Christian walk, I lost sight of God several times. I still do. Ironically, the distance between us grew most while I was working at the church. I faced continual doubts and struggles for decades, long after returning to a life of faith. I am only just now beginning to love God. I am discovering Him in a deeper and far more meaningful way than I ever would have without the separation or questions about my faith. This is a spiritual battle that is far more common than we can imagine. It can affect people new to the faith, or lifelong believers.

I became a prodigal daughter during my journey. As far as I understand it, that means I walked away from my life of faith. I left the church behind and opted to live without the rules of religion or accountability to God. I'm not a biblical scholar, but I always thought the word "prodigal" came into play once the son returned home. Merriam-Webster defines prodigal as a noun, "one who has returned after an absence." Other sources refer to squandering what you are given. I think there's also truth in being labeled as a prodigal upon departure if the reason for leaving is to abandon what is right and pursue what

God would not approve of. Regardless of which definition you choose, it was accurate. I wasn't a prodigal daughter to my family, but I was God's prodigal daughter, as I left Him to live out my desires instead of His.

Acknowledging my status as a prodigal leaves a bitter taste in my mouth. I don't object to it when I hear it used referring to others, and I will celebrate when a prodigal son or daughter returns to God. However, when I apply it to myself, I feel strong undertones of disappointment and shame. It brings an ache in my gut like the repeated thump of the bass drum at a parade. I don't want to be labeled from one specific season of my life. Yes, I walked away from my faith for several years, but I didn't expect a lifetime of living with that identity. The fact that I returned further establishes the label of prodigal. That will always be a part of who I am. Much like a tattoo, that label is a permanent reminder. I will never escape that identity.

I thought I could find the answers to my questions about God on my own. I thought it was up to me to fix this. I was wrong. God protected me during my time away and never stopped loving me. I didn't know it then, but He was putting together the most amazing group of people and situations to show me the way back. I discovered it wasn't about going back to church. God was drawing me to Him this time. Perhaps it was for the first time.

The more I am discovering God's love and growing in a relationship with Him, I sometimes question if I was truly close enough to Him to have left. I left the church, but I'm not so sure I was ever walking in a relationship with God. Sometimes I entertain the thought that maybe I'm not a prodigal after all. Maybe I'm someone who simply never connected with God personally. I know I had a basic understanding and believed in God, but I may have thought it was more about church instead of a relationship with our Father. Even if the technical definition allows for some wiggle room, the general implications of it still apply.

Because I can't escape the label, I am learning to embrace being a prodigal. On one hand, it's a part of my story I'd prefer not to think about. It reminds me of Paul when he speaks in the seventh chapter of Romans about doing the things he didn't want to do. I'm embarrassed that I walked away from God. I imagine a giant label, *Prodigal*, on the wall in large print. It would be caution-tape yellow, bright enough to be the focal point, and remind me to be cautious, as it is a path we can return to so easily. However, I have several other labels I've recently discovered and I'm slowly applying them, overlapping just enough so I can read them all like a collage. A few I've applied so far include *Beloved, Cherished, Forgiven, Valuable, Treasured, Wanted,* and *Rescued*. One of my favorites is *Daughter of the King*. I keep the Prodigal label visible to remind me of my journey, but it is not the one I focus on. I no longer view myself through the veil of disappointment. After all, God never did.

A moment of prayer for all of us

Our dear Father. I have heard people call You God, Lord, Father, Almighty, Dad, or Daddy in their prayers. We are human, and each name used for You may evoke a unique response in us, based on our own life experiences. We know You are all of these, and we thank You for loving us. My prayer is for each person who reads these words to find a name for You that feels comfortable, despite any struggles we may have in approaching You.

Many of us have doubts and insecurities right now, and I ask that You give us the desire to persevere in our search. I pray we can find the labels You give to us. I am praying for all of us to realize for the first time, or to remember, that You are our "why"—You are the purpose in all we do.

We are sorry for the times we lose sight of that, and we are grateful for Your grace to let us try again. We want to draw closer to You. We want to believe confidently in Your love for us. By doing this, we will naturally develop new habits to keep us close to You, and not because they are required or expected.

Our goal is to be so deeply connected to You that You become known by others who can see You in us. Father, we humbly thank You for Jesus. Because of His great sacrifice, we have been restored to You.

It is through Him we pray, Amen.

Chapter 2
Pitchbacks and Slip 'N Slides

IN MY YOUTH, I WAS ALWAYS RUNNING toward one thing or away from another. I had fallen in love with the state of Oregon during family vacations, and long before I was old enough to drive, I knew I would live there someday. I was not a fan of my hometown in the San Joaquin Valley and longed for the day I would leave it behind. I dreamed of heading far away from the dry heat of summers that would start melting a Popsicle before you could get it out of the wrapper or the blazing sun capable of causing sunburns that edged into second-degree. In the winters, the fog was so dense you couldn't see more than inches beyond your hood ornament. Our Tule fog was more than a little extra moisture in the air; it was the stuff of documentaries and multi-car pileups. The wet cold pierced through all layers of clothing, gloves, and scarves, chilling you to the bone. Water vapor saturated the air, dampening your lungs with each breath you took while flooding your nostrils with the trapped smells of your surroundings, whether it be diesel or dirt.

My heart never belonged to a place where the summer slogan was, "but it's a dry heat." The unofficial locals' marketing campaign was, "It's a two-hour drive in any direction to someplace good." Toss in summer temps frequently exceeding 100 degrees and a nickname calling it the "Armpit of California" and you have a better understanding of what I was running from.

I was restless. I had dreams and a plan that took me away from my roots, away from the only place I had known. I was anxious to kick off the cowboy boots and put the orchards and cotton fields in my rearview mirror to head off to the big city. The lure of rain and evergreens was calling me. I had the dream of living in a quirky downtown apartment and working in a high-rise building, maybe even one with a doorman.

My parents had planned on having two children, but to use mom's words, "You were so perfect, we didn't want to risk it." I remained an only child, ending my dream of becoming an aunt. I later would marry an only child, so I never got to be the cool aunt. The tendency to avoid creating trouble remained with me, which is why I feel my story sounds so ordinary. I didn't rock any boats and I am not famous, but I now understand that this is what makes me more relatable than I realized. My life has not been sensational, but it has been remarkable.

I was reading by the age of three and always tested far beyond my current grade level. The first four years of school found me in a new program that blended a few of us into the next grade up in a pod kind of setup. As a kindergartener, I would stay on with the first-grade kids for the afternoons. This continued each year of primary school, spending half of the day in my current grade level class and half in the next grade level up. My learning rate increased. We were called Cubs while at the North Beardsley campus for kindergarten through third grade.

We became proud Beardsley Bears when we entered fourth grade and moved to a much larger campus that was divided between elementary and junior high. The library and cafeteria buildings were in the middle, shared between the two, while also distinguishing the border. When it came time to begin fifth grade, I had my first disappointment related to attending school. I was going to miss the start due to a trip to Hawaii. I know, that sounds rough, doesn't it? My grandparents were on assignment in Honolulu, where my grandfather was leading the project to build the tallest building on Oahu. I had a great time, but I was eager to get back to school because I didn't want to miss anything.

That was the year I had Mrs. Sotelo, a funny and feisty Filipina who taught us about her home country. In addition to our regular coursework, we spent the year trying to master the art of Tinikling, a traditional folk dance from the Philippines. As two people tapped bamboo poles together or on the ground, the dancers would step over them or between them to the rhythm, which sped up as the dance progressed. If you missed your step or weren't quick enough, you'd catch your ankle, and Mrs. Sotelo would giggle and smile after she made sure we were not hurt. I think she even muttered something in Tagalog as she rolled her eyes.

I soaked up school through eighth grade and did well, even maintaining a straight-A record in junior high. The staff and my classmates will always have a place in my heart. This school was so beloved that there are frequent reunions for all previous students, regardless of your graduation year. You will find people in every generation still quoting our motto, "Proud to be a Beardsley Bear." My school experiences were unique because the people felt like family. Most of the kids were together from kindergarten through eighth grade, with only a few new kids coming in.

We were an independent school district with amazing teachers, many of whom were Christians. We had great food in our cafeteria, unlike what we'd heard about the lunches in other school districts. Our annual carnivals were so spectacular, alumni would attend for decades into adulthood. Beardsley's leadership was strong, and most teachers stayed through entire careers; all of this was key to providing high-quality education. It didn't hurt that my dad had been a teacher there until the year I entered school, so some of the faculty knew me, which was pretty cool.

Most of us knew the teachers outside of their school jobs; they were our softball coaches, our neighbors, and our fellow church members. We lived in the same neighborhoods. Mr. Sanford, our principal, and Mr. Francis, our vice-principal, used to go bird hunting with me and my dad. Mr. Francis owned Bakersfield Swim School, where most of the kids at school learned to swim. At 250,000 residents, Bakersfield was not a small town, but it was a small world. We lived in the North of the River (NOR) community and had local parades and community sports leagues. One of my friends, Donna, had my dad as her junior high school teacher. Years later, her father-in-law was my eighth-grade math teacher. See, it was a small world!

The year I graduated from eighth grade, Mrs. Hanley, my reading teacher, became ill and retired. She was always one of my favorite teachers, so I mailed her a card to encourage her. The letter she sent me in response mentioned having tried to call me. Unfortunately, she couldn't reach me, but that kindness still warms my heart. This is but one illustration to show how special it was to be a part of that school. Many of the faculty interactions had a similar personal touch that reflected genuine care for every student. Our school creed, "Think Clearly, Speak Truthfully, Act Nobly" was modeled for us by staff, as was authenticity, a love for people, and acts of kindness.

I dreaded the transition to high school where we would leave our tight-knit class of 130 to become a tiny ripple in a sea of over 2,000 students. I had my plan in place for college, which was to major in accounting and become a CPA. I was ready to get started.

High school is where things took a turn. I had always been a quiet and shy girl. In today's world, I would be labeled as introverted, but back then people called me quiet. The truth is, I lacked self-esteem and felt unwanted. The first day on this huge new campus didn't help things.

My freshman English teacher noticed my name the way most people did. "Lois? Really? As in Lois Lane from Superman?" I was used to that, but then she glanced across the room to one of the popular football jocks and pointed out that James looked like Clark Kent, then wondered aloud if we would ever date. I was mortified. I remember walking into my mechanical drawing class and seeing an expanse of almost forty boys across the large room before spotting one other girl. Yes, ONE! Those two situations etched themselves onto my wall of insecurity that lasted through high school. While I did take college prep courses and was part of the Gifted and Talented Education program, I was only an average student. I don't know what my GPA was, but it wasn't anything spectacular. It no longer mattered to me because I was biding my time and resented having to be there. The way I saw it, life was delayed for four years, and I was frustrated.

Sure, there were some friends, a handful of boyfriends, football games, several remarkable teachers, and a few happy memories I wouldn't have if I'd been able to skip high school. I still think those years derailed me, and the momentum I had going disappeared. When I asked my friend, Tim, recently how he would describe me in high school, he pondered only briefly before stating, "You looked like you were always thinking about something serious." There were some fun times, but this is when life delivered the first actual speed bumps. I lost one friend to leukemia and an adult area youth leader to suicide. My maternal grandmother died. One rainy night, I stood on the side of the road with friends, watching while first responders extracted my cousins, Gaylene and Ronnie, from Gaylene's Mustang, which was wrapped around a telephone pole. For the first time, I had friends who did drugs and drank alcohol while the rest of us worried about them overdosing. Division destroyed the one thing I thought I could count on, my church.

Heading into my junior year, I saw a name on my fall schedule that struck terror in me, Mr. Turk Eliades, affectionately known as Mr. E. Not only was he one of our math teachers, but he was also the golf and football coach. Most of all, he had a reputation that was passed down through generations. He was tough, and he was loud. He would shout at us while rapping our desks with a yardstick. I was fully prepared to drop out of school rather than face a math class with Mr. Eliades. My dad was a firefighter, stationed nearby. One of his co-workers, Duane, had had Mr. E. as a teacher and coach. It took him a while, but he talked me through the tears and anxiety so I could find the courage to step into the classroom. Let's face it, it's not like my parents would have let me drop out anyway.

The saving grace as I crossed the classroom threshold was that I loved math, and I was in the same class with several friends who were similarly quiet. We banded together in fear, but all came to love Mr. E. quickly. A few of us would spend frequent lunch periods in his room, working on extra credit projects and listening to his stories. This is when we realized he was a teddy bear at heart and his shouts and chalkboard eraser-throwing were just a coach's style of passion in his teaching. Our graduation was also the year of his retirement, and four of us wrote a poem together to celebrate. It was not the end of his teaching and mentoring impact, but it was the end of an era for students to experience him in a classroom setting. A few years later, they named the football field for him, complete with a statue!

When I got married, he was unable to attend, but he wanted to make sure we knew how much it meant to him to be invited and how much I meant to him. The store we registered at offered free delivery, but he insisted on dropping our gift off in person. I was heartbroken to know I had missed him when he stopped by. I never got to see him again. Three decades later, I have a white stockpot that I use regularly, always thinking of this wonderful man who hand-delivered it. I will own that pot until the day I die.

I wish I had reached out to him more after high school, as an adult. He would have made an excellent life coach. I am grateful for the influence he had. He is known for sharing this piece of advice with those he coached, and I hope to always remember his words, "You can never play this game again. Live your life to be the best you can be." As we get older, we tend to reflect more. It's a great time to reach out to the people who influenced your life and tell them. I am grateful I was able to write to him and pour out my gratitude and memories before he passed.

My husband, Tracy, had a milestone birthday coming soon. For his fiftieth birthday, I surprised him with a road trip to our hometown, Bakersfield, to see the places that were a part of his childhood. Many places had changed, but several of our favorites were still there. We stopped at one of our favorite restaurants, Hodel's, for our traditional brunch before we headed out on a short side trip to our all-time favorite beach destination on the central California coast. Before we left, I sat in the parking lot, mustered up every ounce of courage I've ever had in my life, and made the phone call to Mr. E. to see if we could visit with him when we came back in a few days. I was afraid he wouldn't remember me.

As I waited for him to answer, I counted each ring, praying for voicemail to answer instead. I was excited, yet apprehensive. My insecurity had me convinced I would have to spend ten minutes explaining who I was, when I was a student, how much he meant to me, who my fellow students were, and why I wanted to stop by. He answered. I panicked. Then I dove into the conversation without breathing between the words, "Hi Mr. Eliades. You probably get this all the time, but I'm a former student from long ago and I just wanted to call and say hi." I gave him my name, and he repeatedly asked me who I was and why I was calling. My heart sank. He couldn't hear me and so the conversation fizzled with me in tears, unable to make the arrangements to go visit with him, and him not knowing I had called. I found out years later that he had new hearing aids and they weren't working correctly.

It would have felt incomplete to write about my high school years without a shout out to Mr. E. Many of my best memories from high school included him. I only wish my husband could have met him, to experience what a dynamic and caring man he was. There are thousands of people who have fond memories of him, spanning generations. He left a legacy when he died. I seldom visit the hometown, but it was gracious timing that put me there the day he died. The family told me he was on the brink of death, so it wasn't a shock. It will always mean so much to have watched the announcement on local news, honoring a veteran and noteworthy man who positively affected so many lives.

Several years before his death, a younger version of him showed up on my front porch 1,000 miles from Bakersfield. His son Jay was vacationing a short distance away from us, and Mr. E. had insisted that he drive over to deliver a personal hello on his behalf. I don't normally open my door if I'm not expecting someone, but I didn't hesitate for one moment when that knock came. I can't explain it to this day, except to think God nudged me to open the door because He was sending me a blessing. He looked and sounded so much like Mr. E. it felt like I had gone back in time. Jay shared a few stories about Mr. E., his health, and recent adventures, as well as a response to the letter I had sent. It was the closest thing to a reunion I would have.

Growing up as an only child, I often related more to adults than my peers. This is a common trait for only children. We also naturally lean toward activities we can do alone. I was an avid reader, loved building and running my model railroad, and put other types of models together. I baked and cooked with Mom and tagged along with Dad no matter what he did—that's what little girls tend to do. When I was quite young, my mom would put me in a dress to play and I would add jeans and cowboy boots before following my dad around. I was a tomboy and enjoyed being outside.

Our town was an active oil-producing region, and you could see pumps at work all around the area. It wasn't uncommon to find pumps enclosed with chain-link fences positioned mere yards from restaurant entrances or alongside roads in town. We had a large oilfield with oil sumps behind our street. The sumps are a series of concentric circles of dirt berms and trails surrounding the pumps, designed to catch the overflow in case of a spill. They certainly provided great places to ride and jump our bicycles and dirt bikes. My friends and I spent a lot of time riding in those oil sumps or the neighborhood streets surrounding them. We lived at the edge of our small neighborhood, just one house away from a cotton field. You could often find me in that field throwing my homemade parachute toy in the air as far as I could, and watching it flutter down. You would never have imagined that much delight could come from a piece of old sheet attached with string to a giant hex nut. I had a Barbie, but most of the time I would bury her in sand using my toy dump truck before rescuing her with my excavator. Another fun note about only children: most of us had a Pitchback to practice softball throws and a Slip 'N Slide or Water Wiggle for summer fun because those didn't require another person.

For a while, we had two horses boarded at a nearby stable. Dad's was a Pinto that stumbled when it walked, but mine was a retired show horse named Lady. She was part Thoroughbred and part Quarter Horse with a beautiful brownish-red shiny coat and a gentle step. I only rode her casually around the track and sometimes the barrels, but in my imagination, I was winning ribbons at the rodeo. I remember taking her to my primary school once for a special outdoor show and tell, along with the goat from the stables.

As a ten-year-old, I was making planters by staining and wrapping wooden clothespin pieces around empty metal peanut cans. I sold them wholesale to a few small gift shops. I didn't amass fortunes, but I felt special walking into the bank to conduct business on my checking account at that age, with dad's co-signature of course. That was the first of several entrepreneurial adventures.

I was fortunate because we didn't have family drama. Each side of the family had groupings of cousins, aunts, uncles, and grandparents, spanning multiple generations. I am grateful to have spent time with all of them throughout the years.

I grew up as an "always there" church kid and loved it. If the doors were open, we were there. Sunday mornings included Bible class and church services. The afternoons alternated between my cousin coming home with me, or me going home with her. In summer, we would swim at the homes of neighbors or soak up the air conditioning while trying to avoid her little brother.

As we grew into our teens, we would often be at the park for a casual church baseball game that included the youth group through the young adults, and those who thought they were still young. We didn't always play, but we felt special being a part of that. We did always join in for the soft-serve ice cream cone or the giant fountain Pepsi with crunchy shaved ice at Foster's Freeze afterward. Those Pepsis were memorable; on a hot summer day, not much tasted better than brain-freezing cold drinks served in a foam cup to eliminate the dilution risk from that glorious ice.

No matter the afternoon activity, it was back to the church building for the evening service. Once a month we had the church potluck afterward. On the best of nights, Ron, from the young marrieds group, would take me and my two cousins to Thrifty's for an ice cream cone. He would put us on the back of his three-wheel motorcycle, a custom-made "trike" with a fiberglass body and a Volkswagen engine. That ride with the air blowing through my hair was the highlight of those nights and probably the most adventurous thing I ever did as a kid.

If there wasn't any kind of special event, our family could be found at home enjoying a home-cooked meal before watching *Mutual of Omaha's Wild Kingdom* and *Walt Disney's Wonderful World of Disney*. Sometimes we'd listen to classic radio programs like *The Shadow* or *Burns and Allen* instead.

Wednesday nights we were at the church building again, often with friends I invited from school. My dad was a deacon and drove the big, retired Greyhound bus to youth events while my mom was a hospitality guru in the church kitchen. My parents did the printing and design work for the bulletins, flyers, and any other special event brochures or posters. One of my favorite projects was the ever-popular church cookbook; I still use mine forty years later. The church was my life. I didn't know anything else. Until I walked away.

Chapter 3
CHURCH KID

THE PATH I TOOK IN MY SPIRITUAL LIFE was not one I could have imagined. I grew up in a quiet, safe, traditional home, and was part of a conservative church family. I believed that this solid, faith-based start would have been the pillar for my entire life, never to shake loose. Those first sixteen years of life could not have provided a more stable foundation for my faith and should have set me up well so I could easily live out Christianity. At the time, it seemed that being a Christian was easy. It was all I knew, so it came effortlessly: go to church, be the most obedient child I could be, and always strive to do the right thing. This was my understanding of living a Christian life. Oh, and try to share my faith with others and save them. Remember, this is the view from the young me. Since I wasn't inclined to take risks or rebel, I certainly couldn't have anticipated my faith wavering. I am confident most who knew me expected nothing less than a life dedicated to God and striving to be the best I could at everything I tried, including living out my faith. In high school, when it was common for students to cut class, I cut French class one time. I immediately reported myself and spent my time in the library. I was not cut out for rebellion or risk.

At church, our family volunteered in a variety of ways. One of my favorites was to help cook or serve the countless meals we made in the newly remodeled industrial kitchen. It was spacious, easily accommodating more than a dozen volunteers, and made it easy to cook meals for youth rallies, Vacation Bible School, and other special events. We had frequent game nights and parties that all seemed to center around food as well. At the monthly potlucks, you knew the food allergies to watch out for, what the favorites were, and who would bring them. Peggy, a dear family friend would usually make my favorite cookie, a soft cake-like treat she called Nerfballs. She'd usually tuck some back in the kitchen for me, just in case I missed it on the buffet line.

The church was family, and as all families do, we had some memorable events. The first time I saw someone get injured, I was quite young. I watched a dear sweet woman, Ruth, fall down the back stairs of the old building. I don't remember being afraid, but I remember being sad for her. She was very calm, but clearly in pain as she sat sprawled across the steps and waited for help. She was one of my favorite ladies in the church and her husband was one of my favorite song leaders.

Once, when I was ten years old, we had the fire department and ambulance show up at one of the potlucks with lights flashing and sirens wailing. Mark, who was severely allergic to nuts, thought a casserole my mom made was topped with mushrooms so didn't think to question it. Mom would never have touched a mushroom and had used walnuts! Yep, Mark had a severe reaction. The medics rushed him away with about a 30-minute window to keep him alive. His newlywed wife, Donna, was still waiting at the hospital forty-five minutes later hoping for an update. Having watched the clock, she feared the internal swelling had killed him. We were thankful when the news came that he would be fine, but he wasn't sure he ever wanted to eat at a potluck again. It's easy to laugh about now, but it is a memory that lasts a lifetime because these people all mattered so much. This was home, these people were my family, and I could not imagine it being any different.

The church had two buildings with a courtyard in the center. There were parking lots at the end of each building, forming a long row on a busy street. The new building included the main auditorium and offices, while the old building had a smaller main meeting room, kitchen, and classrooms. I can still visualize the rooms in both buildings and recall the special swoosh sound of the new building's exterior doors when they closed. This place is in my DNA. As a young girl, I remember the delight in standing over the floor heating vents and watching my dress swirl out around me, filled with warm air puffing it out like a ballgown. It is probably the closest this tomboy ever came to pretending to be a princess.

My dad baptized me in that church building when I was eleven years old. I was terrified of being in front of people, so he baptized me before church, with only my mom present. Now that my faith has matured, I sometimes look back and wonder if I understood what I was doing. My parents tell me they are certain I did, and I wasn't reacting to any form of guilt or pressure from friends or a sermon. Sadly, I can't recall any of this now. I wish I could say that it was a highlight of my life and a memory I will always treasure, but that simply is not true, and that makes me sad. But I do still have my baptism certificate!

The auditorium was large, about forty rows deep, with three full-width sections of pews across, easily accommodating about 600 people. The stage was more than one-third the width of the auditorium, with about six steps elevating it above the floor. It always felt intimidating to be near the front, yet that is where the youth group sat. I can remember feeling so sick during church one Sunday that my cousin Gaylene went to get my dad to carry me outside. Even though I was nearly unconscious, I was concerned about people looking at me as he carried me for what felt like a football field length walk. Remember, my dad was a firefighter. He was carrying me like a rescued accident victim, draped across both of his arms. I was a small teenager at about 100 pounds, but it wasn't like when someone carried a small child vertically over their shoulder. Three things were on my mind, all rooted in fear. Was I going to throw up in the middle of services, in front of so many people? What was wrong with me? Was my skirt tucked up under me, or was I exposing my backside to everyone as he hauled me down the aisle? That last one was my biggest concern.

I was an active and consistent participant in youth group activities, often volunteering as needed. My parents had instilled in me the wondrous joy of serving others. I will forever be grateful to them for modeling this so effortlessly. God was important to me and often in my thoughts. I read and studied the Bible consistently. I prayed regularly. I wanted to tell the world about God and was hopeful everybody around me would become believers, especially some of my favorite teachers. In junior high, I had one teacher I was determined to share Jesus with and would routinely invite to church. Before school, and at lunch, kids could check out all kinds of balls to use on the playground. I worked in the ball checkout room, so I saw Mr. Roberts each day as he came to unlock the door. He was always singing "Ramblin' Rose" and took the time to talk to me before classes began. I connected with Mr. Roberts recently to share the irony of my spiritual wanderings and to offer my appreciation for his patience. I was a kid on fire for God and grew up in a church that taught us to share. I pestered him with invitations to church for an entire year, but I think he must have understood the good heart behind it. We now correspond via email and I plan to take him and his wife to lunch on our next visit.

I remember one man at church, Ken, speaking about sharing our faith with others when he challenged us to "Win One in '81." I was ready for that challenge and began inviting more friends to church. I researched a variety of mission programs and Christian colleges, certain this was the foundation for my life and hoping to make an eternal difference.

In my teen years, our youth group would travel with our leaders to attend regional youth rallies up and down our state, including the San Joaquin Valley and the Greater Los Angeles Area. Little did I know then, but God was putting people into place that would play a role in my life almost forty years later.

I have a lot of memories from my time at that church. Some bring tears while others bring laughter. Some friends of ours, Glen and Peggy, came out to their car once after church to find a brown dog inside, waiting. Apparently, someone dropped him there through their open window. They didn't bat an eye, took him home, and named him Barney. My first experience with a strobe light was at a Halloween haunted house in the classroom wing. With each flash of light, the costumed people would seem to suddenly appear in a different place in the room, leaving me unsure which image was real. It was terrifying because I didn't know where the person was standing; I think this was a significant cause of why I need to be in control of things now.

By the time I was in junior high, I had fallen in love with and knew I would go to Columbia Christian College in Portland, Oregon. The car window sticker I bought at the bookstore on a vacation trip in 1980 still sits on my oak roll-top desk today. I took many of my senior pictures wearing my CCC sweatshirt. I was eager to jump into the next chapter, and that four-year waiting period called high school felt like the longest season of my life.

Church life continued as usual until May 1984, when I heard the first crack come in my spiritual foundation. I didn't realize the extent of the damage at the time; I'm not sure I suspected anything had happened. In retrospect, there is no mistaking it. Ever so faint, deep down in the core within me, hidden from my awareness, was the crack that started the destruction of my faith.

In the blink of an eye, everything that had formed my belief about church was gone. The catalyst for the detour off my spiritual path began with the split of my home church, Oildale Church of Christ. That congregation was the only church home and family I had known, and it was taken from me one fateful Sunday when it broke into pieces. To say it "broke" feels insignificant. I want to use bold letters here in a large font to scream words like shattered and crumbled. It didn't just break. You break a plate, but my church was destroyed, left in tiny fragments, and gone forever.

I remember the Sunday it happened and can still feel the emotional weight that followed if I allow myself to. I was sitting just inside the auditorium on the left side, about four rows in. We normally sat in the front, but for this meeting, we were in the back, and I could see the entire room. I remember some people shouting and I remember other people crying. Elders and deacons resigned. Families divided. Hearts broke. Friendships tore. I definitely remember accusations of false teachings and misunderstandings of intentions. I remember anger and disappointment. What I remember most is a sense of confusion and apprehension. An essay I wrote in college referred to people physically fighting that day. I'm grateful I don't recall that part of it. I have never been close to people in a divorce, but I imagine it feels similar. A divorce of sorts had split up my entire church family.

In the months following, I was sad and was in a near-constant state of crying. I felt so alone without the only church family I'd known. Dolly Parton's song, "I Will Always Love You" was popular on the radio then, as sung by Whitney Houston. Many of the words were hitting my heart regarding the split and the people that were gone. The deepest pain was that our Associate Minister, Denny, and family were moving away. I was seeing a divide within my immediate circle of friends and my own extended family. I was losing so very much at once and they all came to mind when these lyrics would play out. The song is about the heartache of goodbyes, knowing memories are all that's left. There is a lot of gratitude and best wishes in there as well, and that's what we were saying to Denny.

Denny meant a lot to me and was a combination of a minister, an additional fatherly figure, friend, counselor, and brother. I felt close to him and he was a confidant for me at an age when kids don't talk to their parents much. When he left, the circumstances left me feeling abandoned and alone. I don't think anybody understood how much he meant to me, therefore how torn up I was inside. I know I didn't realize it myself until about twenty years later.

I used to babysit their kids and loved that family so deeply. Not only was my church no longer home, but this special family was moving across the country. There was a huge farewell party at Hodel's, a well-known local buffet restaurant, to send them off with a lot of love and support. In my young teen mind, I feared I would never see them again. I remember looking deeply into their son Jason's wide and expressive eyes as they filled with tears, also fearful that we would never see each other again. He was only a little dude, about five, and one of my favorites to babysit. I hugged him so tightly in the Hodel's parking lot as we sent the Boultinghouse family off to their new adventure two time zones east and assured him, "I will never forget you." Our lives grew in different directions, but I was right about one thing. I never forgot him.

God had a future planned for this dear family; a future that had an impact far greater than what could have happened if they had not left Bakersfield. One of the key factors of the church split was an accusation that Denny was teaching grace as the gift from God that saves us, not dependent on our works. I must stand in appreciation of this truth being spoken boldly at a time, in a place, when this wasn't popular. So many of us grew in our faith because of the way he and Philis taught and modeled

God's grace. That split was the catalyst for them moving to Louisiana and launching Image Magazine, a forum that affected many people across the country. Denny and Philis eventually went to work with Howard Publishing, where they continued to share about God's grace. This time it was within the book publishing community and reached tens of thousands, if not more. We needed to know them in our years together so our faith would mature, but then we needed to let them go, to share them with the world.

With the divide behind us, our family and many others started attending the Westside congregation. I was sad and angry, and I resented being there. It wasn't supposed to be this way, and it never grew to feel like home. I never let it. I did my best to avoid any activities I could, and waited, dreaming of the day I would leave for college. There were a handful of friendships, but it was all new and I was the outsider with dreams of leaving the state soon for college. Those I once considered family had betrayed me and it didn't feel like I had anybody to turn to. My cousin was one of my best friends, and she had stayed on the other side of the dividing line and our lifelong friendship dissolved. Bonnie, another one of my best friends, went with her family to a different congregation. With Bonnie, Gaylene, and Denny gone, I felt alone. My parents were there, but I never shared much with them. My youth leaders weren't leading us anymore. I had a new youth minister, but I didn't want to connect much with only one year left of school. I had a few friends, but mostly I counted down the days until departure.

As I launched into adulthood, I did so 1,000 miles north in Portland, Oregon. I was finally a freshman at Columbia Christian College, settled into my dorm room, and ready to meet new people. On the first night of orientation, we gathered in the courtyard, on the cement benches surrounding the water feature with three fountains. With the lights from the fountains reflecting on our faces, the leaders quickly called out those of us from California. We were the ones bundled up in blankets, trying to acclimate to our much cooler new home. I had dreamed of that day since 1980, when I first fell in love with the school and the city. Once again, my environment had set me up perfectly to continue an easy and straightforward walk with God. This was a small Christian college that was based on the same non-denominational church that I grew up in, the church of Christ. I expected it to feel as secure as my home church used to, and it didn't disappoint.

This was my opportunity for a turning point. I was tired of being a quiet, shy, reserved girl who didn't believe she was worthy or valuable. I was tired of feeling like I didn't belong or that I wasn't wanted. I decided it was time to be who I felt I was inside but had always feared to allow to show through. Since there were only three people on campus who knew me, this was my chance for a fresh start. It worked for a while. My personality did a turnaround, and I was happy, active, faith-filled, goal-oriented, outgoing, and well-liked. I taught Bible classes to children at church, where I also worked with the youth group. I was who I had always wanted to be, and more of who I had once been. For what seemed like the first time, I felt accepted by my peers. My self-esteem went from zero to exactly where it needed to be. I was a kind and giving person to anybody who needed me, and I enjoyed helping people again. I was carrying a double major, working part-time, and spending a lot of time working with the church. In addition to the career path I was studying for, I hoped to find someone I wanted to marry. The church taught boys to lead, but teen girls weren't taught much about their roles and opportunities. I had a vision and desire to work as a married team with youth, and I wanted to focus specifically on the girls and encourage them. My faith was strong, my anger and sadness were gone. I thought I had healed from the pain.

The school probably topped out at 200 students, and we knew all faculty members by their first names because we were also attending area churches with them. Sound familiar? This was not your typical college experience where you party, don't study, and goof off. Many of us lived on campus and had a dorm mother and several peer Resident Assistants. There were regular devotionals, daily chapel, and Bible classes. We had deans, ministers, and professors readily available to talk to about God or any faith questions. This all made it easier to live the life of a Christian. We weren't surrounded by foul language or typical college temptations. Everything was in place to keep me on the right track and grow in my faith.

We had some independence, but they expected us to find a church home. I chose Linwood, along with a few of my friends. This is where I was when my faith was rocked by a second loud crack, closer to the surface. This time I felt the rocking below my footing, and it was far more destructive than the first one. I grew up in earthquake country and I have a healthy respect for earthmoving moments. There would be a third quake to hit years later, revealing the full extent of the damage from the first two.

Chapter 4
SOMETHING IS MISSING

IT WAS A SUNDAY THAT BEGAN LIKE ANY OTHER but would change my life forever. I was sitting in Sunday School class next to my friend Dave, more affectionately known as Hoppy, listening as he and the teacher were discussing the Holy Spirit. With undisguised emotion in his voice, Dave started talking about the Holy Spirit being our guide, and how much that meant to him. He was in awe of God's love and filled with gratitude, specifically for the Holy Spirit. He seemed to have such a passionate reverence as he spoke about the power of the Holy Spirit in his own life. I didn't connect with anything being said, and my heart felt empty. As I continued to listen to my friend talk about his love for God and the Holy Spirit, I felt the first nudge of doubt as it poked at my understanding of faith. Sitting in that small classroom, shoulder to shoulder with friends, the sudden realization that church was only a habit for me was overwhelming. It had either always been, or had become, simply a routine.

I began to question if the church, or God, had ever meant anything to me. All three words describing the Trinity sounded foreign to me as I leaned back in my chair, listening to the conversation. I began worrying about my salvation. Holy Spirit. God. Jesus. Each name landed in my heart with a hollow thud, like dropping rocks into an empty well. Nothing in me stirred when I heard them. There was no meaning associated with them, no emotional response, and certainly no sense of gratitude or love. My heart was empty of all emotions about the Holy Spirit, Jesus, and God.

I had listened to sermons all my life and read much of the Bible. I could have explained the most important parts, and I believed all of it to be true. I had filled my head with knowledge, but I couldn't recall having ever experienced an emotional response. The concept of needing God wasn't a part of my way of thinking. I decided I should research why I felt disconnected so I could fix it. I honestly believed it was up to me to figure out what was wrong. It was clear I was not trusting God. I think we all know it was GOD I needed, and this wasn't something I could repair on my own. I found excuses to skip church frequently. When I went, I didn't sing because I felt like a fraud and feared everybody around me would know. I decided to quit taking communion, but I didn't tell anybody what had transpired, and how full of doubt I was.

A few weeks later, the concert group from school, His Heirs, performed at a local church congregation. I was caught off guard when Fred, a dear friend of mine, sang an old Keith Green song I had never heard before. It perfectly summed up how I felt about my faith. In "My Eyes Are Dry" Keith writes of a faith portrayed as being old and empty. The symptoms matched mine, including dry eyes, a hard heart, and cold prayers. As the song continues, it becomes a cry to God, a plea asking how this can change.

BAM! It felt like this song had been written for me. Yes, I grew up in the church, but it was the first time I realized church activities were a routine for me instead of an act of love toward God. I was appalled by that in others while not recognizing it in myself. I always considered my parents to be excellent models of Christianity, and I never doubted their faith was genuine. Until that fateful Sunday, I had never doubted my faith, either. I was no longer certain I had any.

As was common for many who grew up in the church, it didn't feel like I had such big sins in my life to drive me to an awareness of needing God. I was only eleven years old when I became a Christian and my sin level reflected that stage of life. I knew I was a sinner, as we all are, and I needed forgiveness of my sins if I wanted to see Heaven. Now, before you send me emails, I *KNOW* I needed God. It is human nature to categorize sin into levels. I think we do it to make ourselves feel like our sin isn't as bad as the sins of others. You'll sometimes hear people say things about lying on their taxes or taking a pen from the hotel, but then rationalize it by saying it's not like they killed someone.

Well, some people *have* done what some would call bigger sins. If you were to imagine a swinging pendulum on a clock, with God's grace on one side and murder on the other, you'd find lying or stealing much closer to the grace side. It's no secret that we tend to view them as lesser sins. You'd see that it's a full swing to get to the grace of God from murder, but only a short nudge from lying.

Have you known people who have come a long way from sin, what we would call big sins? They are usually overwhelmed with gratitude because they understand how lost they were without God. I think they have a deeper level of appreciation and a clearer understanding of grace. Sometimes I feel a bit jealous of them. I only had petty things that didn't bring that depth of appreciation when I became a Christian. Yes, I know any sin results in separation. There isn't a sliding scale of sin. That's something we've done to make ourselves feel better. I know the Bible talks in Luke about one who has been forgiven little, loving little. That always kind of scared me.

This is when I started noticing the HEART response from those who came from more troubled backgrounds. I compared those responses to my HEAD response of only *knowing* it was the right thing to do. Somewhere along the way, I had stopped feeling anything for God. Maybe I never had any feelings and finally realized it. For me, this lack of feeling was evidenced in the lyrics about the dry eyes, a hard heart, and cold prayers, if there were any prayers at all. My heart was empty. While I was still young, my faith was most certainly old. That song became my mantra and the weight I carried in my heart for years. It still shows up periodically, and apparently will always be there waiting for me in my weakest moments. Satan loves to use our fears and weak spots to hold us down.

I was diagnosed with pneumonia early into my sophomore year. Prior to that, my grades had been excellent, with mostly A's and B's, and it was devastating to watch them plummet after working so hard. When it seemed as if I was going to be unable to recover, I made the agonizing decision to call my parents to take me home. A week later, as I watched my parent's car turn into the dorm parking lot, a powerful sadness washed over me like the ocean's waves destroying a child's sandcastle. The future I had hoped for was ending. I knew I wouldn't return after getting well.

By spring, I had recovered and now faced one of the most difficult moments in my life. I was going to have to let my parents down. I believed I had failed them. I wrote a letter explaining my doubts and my decision to stop going to church. It felt hypocritical to attend, and I was not going back until it meant something to me. I didn't plan to return until I could feel gratitude for God's gift of His Son. My expectation was that this would only be a short time, maybe up to a year. I was wrong.

I opted to not return to college and instead moved into an apartment with a girlfriend from high school. I made a few new friends through work but didn't reconnect with my former church friends. My days were occupied working a customer service job at a local printing company. I filled my evenings playing city league volleyball. During the summer, the evenings were more likely to include friends, movies, swimming, wine coolers, and pizza. A lot of pizza. While I never experienced being drunk, I found that I enjoyed this recent addition of alcohol. I saw friends drink too much and I could understand why my church taught against drinking.

I originally anticipated several months of sleeping in on Sundays. I thought I could fix things with a few conversations with our preacher when I was ready. I did talk to a couple of people that first year, but it was a slippery slope for a young adult on her own. I couldn't tell you when it became a way of life instead of a temporary rebellion. My desire to think about church or God was dwindling.

Have you seen the cartoons which portray the good and bad choices with an angel on one shoulder and a devil on the other, both trying to sway the person's decision? That is exactly what my life felt like.

The little guy with the pitchfork would chant, "It's too late to go back! You aren't a Christian."

On the other shoulder, the one with the shiny halo would lovingly, but sternly, scream, "GO BACK NOW!!!!"

The devil would then taunt me as I slept in on Sundays, "Aren't you enjoying this new freedom and lifestyle?"

To counteract that, the figure in white would declare, "It's been long enough, and you know life will be better. Return before it's too late."

Once again, the pitchfork guy would speak up and rationalize things with, "Oh sure, you're now going to Hell, but this is nice. Have fun."

The angel would then whisper, "God loves you and He misses you."

Eventually, I silenced both voices by announcing that I was in control, not them, and tried to assure all of us I knew what I was doing, even though I did not. I wanted the struggle to end. I wanted the debate to be over. I rationalized everything by telling myself it was only a break from going to church activities and I had accumulated enough points early in life to earn myself some time off.

It didn't take long to conclude something bigger was at the very heart of this. I could no longer picture myself living life as a Christian again. I didn't want to attend church, pray, sing, or read the Bible. I was enjoying the freedom of choice, and the extra free time. I knew I should go back to church, but I still had no emotional desire. I had a fear of the consequences that decision would bring, but I refused to live the same unfeeling and routine life I had lived before. My lifestyle wasn't dramatically changed. I hadn't done anything in complete opposition to how I'd been raised, just skirted it a little bit. But I did believe I couldn't be a Christian unless my heart felt something.

Each spring for almost eighty years, Pepperdine University has welcomed Christians from across the country for the Lectureship. This event features many well-known speakers, primarily from within the Church of Christ community. I attended this several times in the 80s and it was always a small taste of what Heaven must be like. The fellowship was the highlight, and it felt like a reunion each year. It was always such an uplifting event. It was nice to see people from across the region I knew from previous youth events.

I wondered if hearing some of these speakers and connecting with old friends might be helpful. Max Lucado was one of the most well-known preachers and authors in the Church of Christ. He was also one of my favorites and always seemed to have a positive influence. He released his first book in 1985. As I write this now, he has published over forty books and continues to write. He was going to be a keynote speaker. I hoped an emotional shift would be triggered in me by being in that kind of atmosphere and hearing him speak the truth. Nothing happened. I remember feeling so out of place, as if everybody knew I wasn't "one of them." I feared I was at the point where my heart had become so hardened nothing would ever break through. It seemed that this faith I was seeking was never going to become more than routine religious practices for me. While there was something in me that wanted my heart to soften, I didn't know how to make that happen, and my resolve was growing weary.

I longed for others to reach out to me, as I imagined I would if the roles had been reversed. Eventually, I realized that wasn't going to happen, and it was up to me to throw myself a lifeline. Whenever I reached out, friends from church were there to offer words, but I needed them to take the initiative and help me. Most of them probably assumed it was merely a church attendance issue and normal to experience at my age. I knew it was more than that but had given up hope anybody would understand.

I can remember meeting with Garth, the minister at Westside, to talk about why I didn't want to go to church. As I sat across the desk from him, it felt how I imagine it to feel sitting in the school principal's office. He looked me in the eye and nodded as I spoke. I knew he'd heard it before, and it didn't concern him. He seemed to know I'd be back. All he told me was, "You know what to do." Then he quoted Hebrews 10:25 to me, where the writer basically tells us to go to church. He wasn't wrong.

I didn't reach out much during the early years. I sent a couple of letters to area youth leaders I knew and a friend or two from college. I had a handful of people who answered my questions with a lot of Bible verses and shared stories from their own seasons of doubt. Mostly though, I received responses telling me I knew what to do, and they would toss Hebrews 10:25 at me, as if hearing it again would fix it all. I can't tell you how many times I heard that passage referenced. For those of you unfamiliar with this: " . . . not giving up meeting together, as some are in the habit of doing, but encouraging one another—and all the more as you see the Day approaching." (NIV)

My favorites were the versions that started with the stronger words of "Not forsaking . . . " Forsaking? Really? I looked that one up. Abandon, renounce, or give up. I wasn't forsaking the assembly. I was losing my faith and my ability to feel anything!

The second most frequent response was to tell me it would be best if I could find somebody local to talk with. This always left me feeling alone and unwanted. I would vow to stop asking for help, but I didn't know how to progress alone. Gradually, I was losing my ability to persevere and care about anything. I wanted someone to start at ground zero with me and treat me like someone new to meeting God. I didn't know how to ask for that help.

In my wildest imagination, I never would have come up with the idea of a hardened heart, much less known how to soften one. Occasionally, I sensed that it was almost too late for me to return to a walk of faith. Then I'd either go to church or listen to old sermon tapes. Sometimes I'd review the old letters from those who offered support and insights. If I had been consistent in this, I probably would have had a shorter journey back. However, I kept flip-flopping on that pursuit, only reaching out when I became fearful I would never return.

For many years, when I was in junior high and high school, the church in Oildale hosted an annual Spring rally. We would spend almost a week meeting nightly with Doug, a guest song leader from Arkansas, and Jim, a guest preacher from Texas. Jim's sermons were passionate, and he wasn't afraid to challenge us. He encouraged us to think about our faith. I still had the sermon audio tapes from those rallies and dug them out of storage. I was craving a connection to God. I started listening to them again, hoping his words would break the hard shell of my heart and nudge me toward returning to God. It almost worked, and it certainly didn't hurt me. I don't know, maybe it was the Texas accent, but I think it was because he told it like it was. I wanted to experience that kind of tough love; I wanted to be taught and then challenged to act. He would call on his listeners to account for how we were doing with what he just said. I appreciated being challenged, but I wasn't ready to make any changes.

One person who tried to help me the most during this time was my former minister, Denny. Because of his new job in the publishing industry, he would usually be at the Pepperdine Lectureships promoting the magazine each year. Malibu was close enough that he would frequently drive up and spend a few days in Bakersfield visiting friends. I am thankful we never completely lost touch.

I was able to ask him specific Bible questions without being made to feel stupid. He wasn't timid about sharing about grace, or God. He was willing to ask the tough questions to hold me accountable. He knew my journey, and he knew where I was with my doubts, but loved me because God loved him.

Denny is the one who asked me, "Have you turned your back on Jesus?" My response was, "No, I only need time to be away from church and come to my own decisions. I need to make sure this is my faith and not simply a routine handed down to me."

This wasn't a one-time inquiry from him. Regretfully, the time came when I felt I had indeed completely turned away from God, and not just church, and I knew I needed to admit that. If Jesus sat down and told me His story and offered me forgiveness, I believed I would have said, "Thank you, but I'm not interested." I was equally accepting of and frightened by that thought.

I knew I was riding the fence, but I couldn't seem to *want* to get off; it felt safe and comfortable somehow. I believed that if I did not make a decision, I was safe because I had not decided against God. Staying on the fence bought me time. My former youth leader, Ed, told me I needed to choose a side and get off the fence. I also heard this gem that I would kick around from time to time, "No decision is a NO decision." That likely came from Ed, Denny, or both. They were right. I had some great people around me, but my cold heart and stubborn mind were working together to prevent my return to faith. I needed to hear more than, "You know what to do." I felt lost.

It was during this time of walking on my own that I dated a non-Christian for the first time. While that didn't last, I later married his best friend, Tracy. Previously, I would not have considered a single date with a non-Christian, but that was no longer a requirement for me. We were friends first, then the door opened to date. I had purchased a 1974 Datsun 260Z from my uncle and I was excited to show it off. It had a sleek, dark bronze exterior with black leather seats. The ivory vinyl top increased its character, like a French beret perched at an angle. It was exquisite, sleek, fast, and it was mine. You can't simply show somebody a 260Z, you must go out for a spin. That became our first date. I guess he couldn't resist a girl with a fun car!

It wasn't important to me if he had ever considered himself a believer and we never had that discussion until long into married life. One of my biggest regrets in life was choosing to get married while walking without God. You might think it was because of whom I married. That wasn't it.

It wasn't "who married me" but "who married us" that will be at the top of my regret list until I die. Because we were not believers, we didn't want God to be acknowledged as part of the wedding ceremony. We didn't want to include any Bible readings or prayers. The complicated part was that I had childhood dreams of Denny performing my wedding ceremony. In his great wisdom, modeling faith and love, he refused to be the minister at our wedding. This devastated me, and I'm certain it pained him as well.

He didn't refuse because I was marrying an unbeliever, or because of my spiritual state of lost confusion. He simply knew God belonged in marriage, and he especially wanted that for my marriage. This was my first significant consequence of walking away from God. I will carry that grief forever. Denny has since passed so I can't even hold on to the hope of having him speak if we were to renew our vows. There is one thing I can treasure. I was able to tell Denny before he died that I always respected, understood, and admired his decision about the wedding, even though it broke my heart.

Several years into married life, I found myself on the brink of discontinuing the search for God and simply moving on. I thought people were tired of hearing my questions, so I stopped asking. In one last desperate attempt, I reached out to another church friend I hoped I hadn't exhausted already. Phil was a family friend who did a lot of preaching at the small church my grandparents attended in Northern California. I grew to know and love his family through my vacations visiting as a teenager and maintained an email connection with him. I knew he loved me and he had a history of being candid. For a while, we wrote letters and emails, talking through some questions I had. He sent study correspondence and sermon tapes as well.

At one point, Phil met with us to share his faith and study the Bible together, hoping he could help show us the path back to God. I don't remember the details, but I think he knew it was more than a simple church attendance issue at this point for me and we all believed my husband, Tracy, to be a non-believer. While we appreciated the time and love, neither of us was ready to commit to a faith decision. Looking back, I believe this proved to be a time when seeds were being planted in both of us. Phil and his love for us will always have a special place in my heart. I don't think he ever gave up on us.

I wasn't ready to embrace God, or church, yet. Instead, I compartmentalized. I put every letter and sermon tape in a box to be stored away. I parked the decision-making process and focused on the everyday things of life. I kept myself distracted with friends, family, my young marriage, and my work. I stuffed that box into the back of a storage closet and I pushed all thoughts of God into the back recesses of my mind.

Chapter 5
WELCOME HOME

AS WE SAT IN OUR SMALL RENTAL HOME in late summer, trying not to move more than necessary for fear of overheating, I decided it was time to introduce my husband to the delightful Oregon summers. We didn't have air conditioning, but our swamp cooler was gurgling water, trying to cool the air it would blow into the house. Accompanied by the droning whir of the swamp cooler fan, I began to verbally paint a picture for him of lush green trees and lawns, with gigantic mountains looming against the backdrop of colorful sunrises. I reminisced about evening walks requiring a sweater to ward off the cool breeze and beaches that wouldn't scorch your feet.

He put in for vacation the next day, and with the intolerable Bakersfield heat bearing down on us, I threw together an impromptu vacation to the land of cooler temperatures. A few days later, we left temperatures exceeding 100 degrees and headed to Portland. We were not disappointed to be greeted by double-digit high temperatures with the first digit being an eight. It worked; he was hooked on the beautiful scenery and cooler weather.

He lost his job one year later and we seized the opportunity for a new adventure. We hit the highway with some friends and headed north for a few days. On that quick visit, we secured a house to rent and connected with a temporary employment agency for jobs. All that remained was to return home, sell off the excess belongings, say our goodbyes, and rent an enormous moving truck so we could begin the next chapter in our lives. I had no way of knowing this would be the first step in returning home to God.

Less than thirty days later, the truck and our car were ready to caravan, full of all our belongings that awaited a new chapter. Tracy drove the big truck, and I had our dog to keep me company in our car. We spent the first night with my grandparents, just east of Sacramento. The next day would bring our longest day of driving. We encountered a heavy downpour in the Mt. Shasta area that left us shaken. When the windshield wipers refused to push any water aside, it was time to pull over and wait it out. I wasn't convinced our windshield wasn't going to crack from the pounding rain. That storm delayed our arrival time, pushing us toward nightfall. Hours later, with a sigh of deep relief, we finally saw the Portland city limits sign.

After navigating through narrow neighborhood streets and taking out a small tree branch, we parked our 24-foot moving truck in front of the rental house. We approached the door with our key in hand. As we inserted it into the lock, apprehension creeped in like the shadows crawling down a dark granite wall at nightfall. I don't know if it was the fatigue of the trip, the real-life crime shows we watched on television, or the fear that it went too well to be real, but we were suddenly feeling unsure. Would the key fit? Was the person who rented the house to us the owner? Had we become victims of a scam?

The key turned and we were in! Complete darkness greeted us along with the most atrocious smell we have ever encountered. There were no light switches or overhead lighting in the main living areas. We stumbled our way through the darkness of the first two rooms to the kitchen before we found a switch to try. With the upward flick of the wrist, a small old-fashioned pendant light offered a dim yellow glow. We still didn't know what caused the smell and began to wonder if that was why it had been so easy to rent. This was an old house, built in 1915. It had a lot of character, with an archway between the living room and dining room and a fabulous built-in hutch. The kitchen was the third room straight in. To the right of the dining room was a walkway to the two bedrooms and bathroom. An old porch was enclosed at the back of the house to make an extra room.

We unloaded the bare essentials, the mattress, and television and drove through the closest Kentucky Fried Chicken. Returning home, we settled onto the mattress on the cold, hardwood floor with our bucket of chicken beside us for a picnic. We found something to watch on the television, also on the floor, to distract us from the unfamiliar surroundings and apprehension. Our dog paced from room to room, uttering the occasional random growl. During the night it began to rain and we were startled awake by a deafening noise pounding all around us. Complete doubt was now sweeping in. We wondered what we had gotten ourselves into with a house that smelled bad and made strange noises. Even our dog was nervous, or he simply missed the softness and quiet of carpeting.

Within a week, we had confirmed the rental was legitimate and we had not been scammed. We eventually discovered the smell was coming from upstream where the pulp mill would spew an obnoxious odor that wafted clear into town a handful of times per year. The house sat empty for a few weeks before we arrived, so the smell had settled in without any way of escape. It turned out the rattling was the rain gutters, a sound we now enjoy but had never experienced before in our dry climate.

We gradually found our new rhythm, consisting mostly of work and trying to learn our surroundings. Where were the grocery stores? What part of town should we avoid? Where do we want to eat? There were no more extended family dinners and celebrations, no backyard barbecues with friends and neighbors. It was just us. We settled into permanent jobs and found friendship with a neighbor couple.

Eighteen months later, our landlord informed us she was selling the house. We had two months to find a new place or buy it from her. We had no intention of purchasing a home yet. After making a few pros and cons lists, we had our answer, and a mortgage loan. We purchased our first home without the excitement, or hassle, of packing and unpacking. It felt anti-climactic to not have a moving day with paint projects, moving boxes stacked up, and meals on paper plates. There was no fanfare, just a new debt.

Without the time-filling distractions of friends, family, and my old routines, it was clear something bigger was missing than people and activities. While I had a great job and we had purchased our first home, I felt empty and aimless. I realized that at the relatively young age of thirty-two, I was simply waiting for life to run its course. I no longer had my old support system around me and it was too soon for new friends to become the people you can go deeper with. I was unsure where to turn.

I remembered a long-ago heard sermon from Jim, the Texas preacher, about our "God-shaped vacuum" that only He could fill. I found the tapes in a box stuffed far up in the attic and started listening to them again, trying to fight my way back to faith. I was lonely and just desperate enough to pursue answers one more time. Fearing he wouldn't remember me, I reached out to Jim via email. He graciously sent me some additional sermon tapes and we messaged back and forth addressing some of my questions. I had lost much of my basic Bible knowledge and doubt replaced it. I had to go back to the beginning and accept that God does exist, the Bible is real, and the story of Jesus is real. Although Jim was halfway across the country, he knew two women, Deanna and Kristy, in my city and introduced us to each other via email.

Deanna and Kristy quickly became two of my friends and encouragers along this journey. They were among the first people I connected with in Portland from a Christian background. While they didn't live nearby, and we never went to church together, we spoke about God and their faith.

I invited them to dinner once, so they were able to meet Tracy. We used to have people around all the time, and I missed that fellowship. I was so excited to have guests coming. I dusted the house and straightened all the pictures. I even coached the dog on how to be polite. I made one of my favorite meals, a BBQ brisket with a full range of side dishes. It slow cooks for eight hours so the fragrance of sweet smokiness permeated the house, drawing you in and making your mouth water.

We gathered around our little antique maple dining table that once belonged to my grandmother, and I nervously asked them to say a prayer. We passed all the dishes around family-style, filled the iced tea glasses, and placed the cloth napkins on our laps. After hours of cooking and a round of nervousness to serve new friends, we all took one bite and stopped mid-chew, unable to swallow the salty meat. We ordered a pizza and put away the side dishes. I was so embarrassed.

After they left, I found the other half of the roast in the freezer and discovered the butcher had given me a *corned* beef brisket instead of a regular beef brisket. Corned beef has a high salt content and is a completely different kind of meat. When you combined that with the seasonings I added, the meat was rendered inedible. I'm not sure if they ever came back for dinner or if we always met at restaurants from there out. Those lovely ladies accompanied me for a season, played an important role in my journey, and remained in contact. They have both moved away, but I keep them on my list of people I will visit if I travel to their area. They were a comfort from God and an encouragement to continue searching.

While I wasn't ready to admit it, I knew God was the answer I was seeking. I did the only thing I knew to do and started visiting a few of the local churches I had known from my college days. I had changed though, and they didn't resonate with me. Nor could I feel God drawing me to them. I started with the one I knew best, Linwood, the church I attended while in college. This was the same church building I was in when I first questioned my faith. I had not been there for thirteen years, but it immediately felt familiar.

Church buildings seem to have a signature smell, within denominations. The familiar scent from Churches of Christ seems to blend carpet, wood pews, upholstery, grape juice, perfume, aftershave, potluck spills, and the pages of the hymnals together into a comforting reminder of my youth. I had walked in on a busy Sunday morning before church began. I intended to be a few minutes late so I could slip in unnoticed, but traffic was light and my plan had failed me. I listened to the frenetic buzz of conversation and laughter, while not meeting anybody's eyes. I spotted the member photo wall. It was the same wall as before, and it brought a flash of panic. This traditional church is what I left. As I glanced around the foyer, I saw a room filled with church people I didn't know, hugging each other, and having conversations I wasn't meant to be a part of. This outlier status is why I left. I turned around and walked out. Sorry, Linwood, it wasn't meant to be. I didn't belong there now.

Several months later I connected with my college friend Fred, and we visited church with him and his wife. I was stunned to walk in and see another familiar face. I knew the worship leader from when I was in junior high. On the stage, there was Jeffrey, more than 1,000 miles away from where I'd last seen him almost twenty years before.

That church felt comfortable. It held most of the same doctrinal beliefs and practices I was familiar with, but the slight differences were refreshing. This church used musical instruments, while I came from an a cappella background, and they allowed women to pray publicly, which was strictly forbidden. A strong, passionate love and commitment to God came through from the worship and praise team, the various pastors, and others who led during services. It seemed that I might find people there I could approach with questions and not be judged.

One person particularly inspired me from the first time he prayed. In him, I immediately recognized a deep sincerity and a transparent desire to live a life committed to serving God. It turned out Kurt was one of the ministers. He was noticeably different from what I was used to seeing in people who went to church only as a habit or obligation. That intrigued me. The way he said things when he taught, and the warmth of his prayers moved me. I was nervous, but I reached out through email.

He was a great sounding board for my questions and played a significant role in my journey back to faith. We had a lot of great question-and-answer email conversations and a handful of lunches where he would meet with me and Tracy near our workplace. Another friend was studying with us as well and it wasn't long before I was attending two different church services back-to-back each Sunday. One felt comfortable because it was the same non-denominational church I grew up attending. The other one felt fresh and stretched me beyond the confines of my upbringing. Tracy was not attending church with me, but I knew I needed to be there.

I had officially started my journey to find God again. He placed a team of unlikely people around me, most of whom I never would have met had I not walked away from church in the first place. My non-denominational upbringing instilled in me the belief that denominations were not considered theologically sound. It felt strange to seek spiritual guidance from outside the Church of Christ. Ironically, most of the people who played the biggest roles in directing me back to God were people I never would have considered talking to before.

The more I searched, the more questions I had. I could find a verse in the Bible that condemned something and assume it was aimed at me. I struggled with the validity of my baptism, questioned if I'd committed the unpardonable sin, and wondered if it could be as simple as a choice to return to God. Was I ever saved? Was I still saved? Why didn't I feel anything about God? I was afraid to make any decisions and get locked into church again. I enjoyed having my weekends free and it was nice to not feel obligated to people or schedules.

Denny was always available to answer questions and he was not afraid to be direct with me or challenge me to think through what I was saying. He was quick to remind me to, "Go to the cross. It's all about the cross." His understanding of grace was exquisite, and he wanted everyone he knew to grasp the fullness of it. We continued to correspond regularly through this time. Often, an unexpected package would arrive with books and CDs he thought would encourage me. There was always a brief note reminding me that God loved me and of course, "Remember the cross."

Music has always played an important role and frequently goes straight to my heart. There was one Sunday when the musical worship at my second church,

Mt. Scott, was particularly impactful. I couldn't ignore the need to act upon my emotions. I jotted a quick note to Brent, the worship pastor, and shared how meaningful the musical worship had been. I asked a couple of corresponding questions about the songs and provided my email address so I could avoid a verbal conversation.

I would frequently stop in at the building during the week to spend some quiet time in the sanctuary. It was a great place to connect with God in an atmosphere that allowed for solitude. I was getting to know the church secretary enough to say hello and wave as I walked through the lobby, and no longer had to explain why I was there. As I approached the office to say hello and drop off the note, I noticed her desk was empty although the door was open. I approached the door with the intention of dropping it on her desk before heading to the sanctuary. God had other plans. For the first time in all my visits, He put Brent square in front of me when I walked in, instead of the church secretary. Brent insisted on reading my note while I waited. I was anxiously trying to wish my way into disappearing. We then sat and talked for over an hour.

Because he didn't know me, he couldn't make assumptions. Even after learning I had grown up in the church and knew what I needed to know, He didn't skip ahead or tell me I knew what to do. I think I needed to start from scratch, and somehow, he sensed that. I longed for someone to talk to me as if I'd never gone to church. Brent was the first person to do that. I hoped that kind of fresh start would help me see the gift of Jesus in a new light. I wanted it to mean something to me.

I spent the next few months meeting regularly with Brent to continue the conversation. One day he issued a challenge as he prayed over me. I was busy trying to find answers to my questions, which proved to be a distraction. He thought I needed to confess to God, to remove my apprehension toward God, and he gave me a deadline to reach for. My response, as noted below, has stayed with me since then and frequently continues to nudge me.

"In your prayer on Friday you asked that I'd be able to confess my sins of turning away from God thirteen years ago. You asked me to do that before sundown. Let me tell you, you are so right about the devil occupying our time and distracting us from what we need to do. I went into the sanctuary after our meeting and tried to pray about this, but I wasn't ready to complete it. During the drive home that evening, I watched the sun set and felt much the same way Peter must have felt when he heard the rooster crow, having denied Jesus three times. I still haven't addressed this, but plan to this week. I know I won't be able to move any closer to God if I'm still trying to hide from Him."

During our meetings, he continued to shed light on things I had yet to see as playing a role. One of the best things I've ever done was complete a workbook with him, *Through the Wilderness: Finding God's Presence When All Seems Lost* by Carol A. Brown. This took me to places I had not yet discovered, nor could have imagined, and carried me a long way toward returning home to my Father God. This is the book I refer to in this journal entry from a letter I sent to him later.

"As I shared with you Friday, I never realized my disillusionment began when my home congregation split up. I never understood that it was disillusionment, I thought it was doubt, and I always thought it started in college. It does make sense that the wilderness search began when my church split. You're right, I didn't have the trust in God to call on Him during that time. It was already too late for that. I've read through the first four chapters and done the workbook for those. It's clear to me that I never had a trust in God or a personal relationship/walk with Him. I knew about God and I confessed His name, received Him in my heart, and was baptized. Unfortunately, I never learned to trust Him. No wonder I blamed Him when Oildale split up! I think I may have unknowingly had my trust in the church instead. It's possible I had faith in God but didn't let trust play a role at all.

Welcome Home

Tonight, I kneeled at the altar and prayed about the forgiveness of those folks who caused the split. What a great idea! You were quite right. I still harbored resentment and anger toward them. For many years afterward, I told myself I wouldn't stop to help the two guys who caused the split if we were in the desert and I was driving a water tanker. That, I'm sad to say, is a pretty strong case of hatred and I'm ashamed that it was a part of me.

When I left the church, it all seemed to go by the wayside. Or so I thought. Now I see that it's still very much a part of my heart and had only been buried and ignored. My heart and soul feel so much lighter now that I've forgiven them and asked for forgiveness from God for my feelings toward them. It's an amazing and beautiful thing what thirty minutes of deep, humble, tearful prayer can do. I tried your suggestion of kneeling, and that increased the power of it. I'd been blaming God for what happened, and I needed to clear the air with Him. I feel like I can now move on to the next step I need to take. Progress is a wonderful thing, even when it's painful."

I was fortunate to have several people surrounding me to answer my questions and wait for me to find my way. Then they would answer more questions. After six months of seeking, I took the time to summarize where things stood, believing this would help me know with certainty before taking an ultimate step of faith. I am a detailed person and I wanted to make sure I didn't leave anything out. I didn't want to go through any doubts down the road again. This is the summary straight from my notes in my journal.

Belief in God

I believe in God and I believe He created me. I believe He will take care of me if I let Him, but that He will allow me to take the controls and act out of my own decisions. I often use the image of Him wrapping His arms around me and holding me while the storms pass by. This belief in God creates a soothing feeling, and I'm starting to feel comfortable talking about God. I have started to pray to God to thank Him for the people around me or to pray on their behalf. Sometimes I share my feelings about my journey home or ask for His help in this effort. I asked Him to guide me to someone that He will use to reach me, to give me an open heart to what He's saying to me. I often ask Him to change my heart so I can feel like I can draw near to Him. I tell Him I want *to want* to feel repentant and that I want to come back home.

Belief in Jesus

On a good day, I believe Jesus is the Son of God. I believe God did send Jesus to be our Savior, to bear the burden of my sin. When I read the story of the cross, I am overwhelmed at what He was willing to endure for me. I never realized the suffering He went through before. Perhaps I never understood that Jesus experienced that as a human.

However, sometimes I find myself questioning the account of Jesus's life. Not the fact that He was a man, I can accept that He existed. If I'm in the right frame of mind, I can believe the entire story. But if I'm not, and I look at it strictly from a worldly standpoint, it still seems a little "too much to accept." It does seem a little over the top sometimes that a man could do the things claimed in the Bible. Miracles and healing seem far-fetched. The thought that someone would suffer and die, or that people would follow. It sounds extremely unlikely to me.

Changing My Life

When I reflect on the cross, it almost always brings me to my knees in shame and disgust that He was willing to be killed in that manner for me. Yet I remain unwilling to give up my life. I'm having a difficult time understanding why I don't want to let go of my sins and my life. I'm not proud of my sins. I am proud of who I am today, but I also realize that pride can be a sin, so it's confusing. I think it's that I enjoy being in control of things, it's what I'm used to. Whether it's at home or in my job, I've always been the one to take care of things. It's exceedingly difficult to humble myself and let go of the reins. Life isn't all that bad so I don't think I need to let go.

Sometimes I think I must not love God if I can't accept this gift of grace He's offered. Who in their right mind wouldn't gladly give up a few lousy habits like skipping church or watching inappropriate movies in exchange for a gift so amazing? Is it such a bad thing to stop the occasional swearing or envy? Does this mean I don't fully understand this gift? I acknowledge that it's a selfish attitude, but I don't have any emotions about Jesus and what He did for me.

Yes, I can say the words "I'm grateful", but I can't FEEL the gratitude. Since there are no feelings of gratitude, there are no feelings of wanting to give everything up to follow Him. At church, I watch these people that are so full of love and appreciation for God, and I don't understand it. I want to feel the desire to change, but I'm still waiting for that to come. I don't think any more progress can happen until I reach this point.

I have had an extremely difficult time wrestling with the total lack of feelings issue. I can't seem to let go of the expectation that a response to Him should come when I feel something so intensely, that it stirs me to action. Yet I also understand that I need to focus on the faith part and allow the feelings to come in response. I'm so concerned that it's not real if I don't feel it. That's what started this entire season of walking away. I can't go through those doubts again.

AHA! Moments

I've come to realize that I'm looking for this missing person who is lost inside of me who used to have a firm belief in God. I've been looking for that person, but I know now that she is gone. Instead of trying to find who I used to be, I need to start over.

I need to focus on admitting I can't do this alone, and I'm not going to pretend that I can anymore. I did need to be honest with God and tell Him that I wasn't doing a great job being in control and everything was not all right. I know that I do need God more than ever.

I've heard songs about God being more than a story or a feeling. I want to feel this way about God. I want to have a passion for God and what He did. While I'm tired of not feeling, I need to accept that God doesn't require feelings, just my whole heart. This is critical to progress.

I have become fascinated with the concept of grace for the first time in my life. I can feel the pull to come home to God. I long to feel that I can return. I want to find my way back home. I dream about the day I will fall to my knees at the feet of God and be loved like never before.

I want to be loved by a God who will run to me when He sees me and sweep me up in His arms. I believe it will happen once I can decide. I didn't know I craved that kind of love and acceptance, that I needed that love.

Peace and Rest

I was feeling the frustration and exhaustion of working so hard on this decision. Imagine that. I was working on it as if my actions were going to save me. I've learned a couple of key things here. First, I have to allow God to work in His timeframe. Second, it's ok to rest. I see now that I needed to rest, and that God would protect me and hold me during this time so I could press on in my search. Denny once shared the most beautiful image of God singing over me while I rested. I have changed the direction of my prayers to reflect my willingness to allow God to control the timeframe. I think that is trusting God.

January 25, 2001. Eight months of study, prayer, church, counseling, buckets of tears, frustration, and a group of unexpected people around me I believe only God could have orchestrated. This led to the day I again believed who Jesus is and why I'm important to Him. I ran back into my Father's waiting arms and decided to accept God's amazing gift of grace once again. Additionally, I chose to completely surrender my will to Him, perhaps for the first time. Somehow, my initial expectation of a year or less to figure things out and take a break from church ran a little longer than I anticipated. That stretched into thirteen years of wandering in my self-imposed desert. It felt good to be home.

It was an important moment in my life that was made more memorable the instant it concluded. I had made arrangements with the office manager at church to use the prayer chapel for me and a friend to meet and talk through more questions. We spent a few hours sitting on the couch in the chapel, going through every last detail so I could be sure I'd done my research. We looked up scriptures, we prayed, and I cried. I went through my checklist of questions to clarify the answers to and verified my understanding. The east wall of the prayer chapel was a life-sized mural of Jesus in the fields with sheep. The angle of His face always made it seem like you were being watched. Truly, the two of us studying that night weren't alone. God is always present and that was evident that evening. There was only one thing left to do. I needed to make a decision.

While we were meeting, the security guy verified the door was locked but did not check to see if the room was occupied. Moments after I rededicated my life to God, we stepped out into the hallway to be greeted with blaring sirens from the alarm. I chuckle to think maybe that was God celebrating!

Here's a fun fact. Steven Curtis Chapman had a popular song that year called "Dive." It was an upbeat tune that always caught my ear when it played, but I didn't feel I could sing the lyrics because it wasn't true for me. It described a life of going all in, being willing to dive deep, and take a leap of faith. I used some of the lyrics as part of my statement of faith that night to confirm my decision to return to walking with God in surrender.

Section Two

The Perfect Job for an Imperfect Person

Who I Became

God, you waited for me to discover that my approach to faith is unique, and that this is okay. You waited for me to understand that You never wanted me to conform to those around me. You waited for me to know that even when the wind blows, I can stand firm in faith. You waited for me to realize I was resilient by allowing the storms that would bend me without breaking, much like a palm tree. You waited for me to accept that I am stronger than I believed.

Thank you for waiting.

Chapter 6

WOULD YOU LIKE TO WORK HERE?

WITH MY FAITH ON A SOLID FOUNDATION again, I was ready and eager to begin rebuilding my church experience. I had been away for a long time and I was anxious to find my role in this new congregation. I was excited to volunteer and curious to discover how I would be serving. I started my Sundays at the early service in what would become my home church. When the closing "Amen" came, I could rush out and just make it across town to Mt. Scott for their late service. Tracy wasn't attending either church with me. It wasn't long before I was volunteering at both churches during the week. Mt. Scott was different from what I was used to, but it was challenging me and feeding my new hunger for God. I didn't know many of the songs, the baptism belief wasn't what I grew up with, and they allowed women to preach. The doctrinal differences were significant and would prevent me from ever calling it home. Perhaps because it was different, I was more open-minded, and I found my faith was growing stronger because of my time there. I wasn't ready to stop attending and continued to visit off and on for a few years.

At my home church, I volunteered with Kurt, the Minister of Spiritual Maturity, and his assistant, Helen. This continued for two years until she resigned. I had been praying for an opportunity to work there because I wanted to be more than a part-time volunteer. I was getting to know the staff and the inner workings of the church. I hoped to become a part of this team. I was particularly drawn to the ministries Kurt led and the unique way he served God. I wanted to support him in his work because it resonated with me. Many of the ministry areas he led filled the very gaps I experienced growing up in church. It was fulfilling to see people being encouraged to grow in their faith. I always understood the purpose of missions to other countries, but it bothered me when the church never seemed to care about teaching others in our country. I had also only experienced churches counting those they saved but never teaching them how to live out a life of faith.

Kurt and I met weekly to review projects and touch base. On the first day of April 2001, I arrived early, only to find his office empty. As I waited, I began to feel a bit left out, as I listened to laughter billowing from down the hall. The staff was gathered in the conference room around the corner, celebrating a birthday. I could see many of them peeling back cupcake liners on their treats while walking back to their offices. I felt alone and outside of it all. Mostly, I wanted a cupcake. Years later, I was told the rest of the story. Before the wonderful cupcakes I saw them enjoying, they were given cupcakes that were meatloaf in disguise as a trick played on the staff by the bookkeeper's best friend. It was a tradition to prank the bookkeeper on her April Fools' Day birthday, but this time they turned it back on the staff. Once I knew that, I didn't feel so bad about being left out and I'm glad they were able to enjoy a real treat afterward. Anybody that got frosted meatloaf instead of cake certainly deserved something yummy.

The job opening came when Helen's husband died two years later. She had to seek full-time employment, so she resigned. Logically, I knew it wasn't my fault and it wasn't a direct result of my prayers that her husband died. Still, it felt weird for a death to be the turning point that landed me my dream job. In the back of my mind, I always felt a little sorry I had prayed for the job. They didn't advertise the open position. I was asked if I'd like to work there. I mean, come on, did they really need to ask?

I was being invited to join others in a job where you get to spend all day hanging out with God and praying with co-workers. I painted a fully illustrated fairy-tale image in my mind. Joy would be hanging from the rafters like glittery streamers as love swirled around my every step. Cute songbirds were going to flit beside me, chirping positive thoughts and creating a beautiful melody. Naturally, I expected praise and worship music would play in the background of life at this glorious job. I assumed there was going to be daily staff morning devotionals and prayers. I anticipated being surrounded with an abundance of spiritual fruit like peace, joy, and love, as described in Galatians 5:22-23.

I was going to be used by God! I would fulfill my purpose on this earth, make a difference to the lost world, and help bring the members of the congregation into a deeper relationship with God. I was going to get to spend all day, every single day, loving people and caring for them. This had to be the best job in the entire world. Right? Oh wait, and they will pay me? OK, let's be honest. The pay was nowhere near what I was used to, and I could have made more flipping burgers. But this was special. This was the perfect job. This was God calling me. My answer was a resounding, "YES, OF COURSE I WANT TO WORK HERE!"

Accepting the job was a simple decision. Choosing to work for less than half my pay scale made it a family decision. Financially, it would be a sacrifice for us if I took this job instead of staying in the business world. However, I was afforded great flexibility with the schedule and there was a calming peace and a clear sense of purpose that came with the job. After years in the corporate world, the emotional benefits of this opportunity looked to outweigh the financial loss. I was able to say, "Yes" with my husband's full support. We both knew a life of service was what I had been guided to.

In May 2003, my church employment began with my swift and sure signature on a W-4 form. For the third time, I was placed where it should have been easy to follow God. Growing up in the church and attending a Christian college may have appeared to set me up for faith, but we know how that turned out. With my renewed dedication and a certainty that my faith wasn't inherited, I was going to be spending my days working at a church. This seemed like the best way to deepen my faith and keep me on track. I never could have anticipated the impact the job would have on my life.

It wasn't long before I realized my new role wasn't the glowing, shiny opportunity from Heaven I naïvely anticipated. Like badly grown out hair coloring, the roots under that glow began to show. Beneath the shine, I saw a job like any other. In my fantasy world, training would have been lengthy and detailed. Instead, it was like most other jobs. I had a few hours of training, but then it was the usual but unspoken, "Here are the basics you need to know. You'll sink or swim. You're on your own. Good luck!" This should have been my first hint that it wasn't any different from the corporate world I knew. I missed that clue.

Chapter 7
DOES GOD ATTEND STAFF MEETINGS?

LIKE MOST NEW EMPLOYEES, I WAS EXCITED for the opportunity and eagerly anticipated each new part of the job. I knew I was working somewhere unique and recognized it as a special opportunity to serve God and an entire church congregation. I held a lot of respect for the job I was embarking on and I had high expectations that this ministry was a calling. I was fresh enough to church life to still have that grand vision of what I expected as I walked into my first staff meeting.

Realistically, I didn't have a clue what to expect outside of my own imagination and hopes. Nobody had given me an agenda so I could be prepared ahead of time. I did think a church staff meeting would be different from those in the business world. I felt humbled and honored to be a part of God's team, a part of a staff that was going to move mountains for God. In the beginning, it was a muted version of what I anticipated. A typical staff meeting included time spent reading through the prayer requests from Sunday, taking note of surgeries, deaths, and other significant life events needing pastoral care. If any of us had something going on personally, we could share our requests. Almost every meeting included our senior pastor asking the church secretary, Linda, to write something down to remind him to do later. She wasn't his personal assistant but seemed to be the one he leaned on for everything.

We would spend time checking on people, ministry updates, worship schedule details, and other operational concerns for keeping a church running smoothly and effectively. These weren't traditional staff meetings, but mostly prayer meetings with a touch of business. It seemed appropriate since we were meeting in the same prayer chapel where I made my decision to come back to God. The mural of Jesus watching was a part of every meeting as we sat in chairs, forming a rectangle around the room's perimeter. Sometimes one person would lead a prayer, but usually we would break up into smaller groups to pray after the meeting. The men would pair off, but the women would stay as one group for this prayer time. The pastoral staff would meet later for the business side of things. The support staff might or might not be informed about those details unless we had an assignment.

Does God Attend Staff Meetings?

A few years later, we progressed into a combined staff and prayer meeting. This was helpful because we didn't need to rely on our bosses for information updates. By this time, my job had expanded to include working for Jon, the youth pastor, so I had two ministries to keep track of. This new format was wonderful for me because neither of my two bosses were great with communicating the little, but pertinent details. However, this is when I started to realize the shiny halo I had placed on the job was starting to dull.

I imagined church staff meetings would be a time of connection. I thought they might even include a brief time of study and prayer with a little worship music thrown in before we got to the business side of things.

I expected to have discussions about how to help our members grow in their faith, love God deeper, and find unity with each other. I wondered how we would plan for the months ahead to unite ministries and develop strong cross-generational relationships. I was sure we would discover innovative ways to show God's love to more people and help them find their place to serve. I earnestly hoped our staff meetings would be filled with purpose, God's purpose, and would help to fulfill His grand vision.

As it turns out, the church staff meeting was filled with purpose all right, but it was usually each individual ministry or staff member's purpose. Oh, I know God was there, but it didn't seem to me as if He was often invited to speak into the plans we made. I thought it seemed more like we invited Him to bless the plans we made for His church. I didn't think that's what He had in mind. I still don't. I'm not saying any of our staff members had bad intentions. God wasn't always an afterthought. I simply wasn't expecting it to be so normal. People are people, and those on a church staff are no different. We were ordinary people, and people are often fueled by their own desires.

To be fair, I guess we were all simply doing our jobs and striving to create the best ministries we could. But it wasn't always happening in the manner I believed God would have wanted to see, or what I expected. Remember, I thought we'd have devotional readings and songs before each meeting.

While each person was responsible for their area of ministry, it saddened me greatly to see the lack of combined focus on the one reason we were there: to connect people with God. I felt like the ministries and programs had become the primary purpose. The priority behind each ministry was to serve God and to root people deeper in their faith. Don't misunderstand me here, the heart behind most of this was solid. But I had failed to see that a church is like any other business, with individuals in charge of departments.

DOES GOD ATTEND STAFF MEETINGS?

Calendar meetings were the worst of all. Not only did they start a couple of hours earlier in the morning than when my mind became alert, they lasted for hours. Oh, and because they started earlier, I was always starving because I didn't take time to eat breakfast. Our staff was divided into ministry staff and support staff. When a calendar meeting was announced, you could almost hear the eyes rolling from the support staff. We knew this was going to be a three-hour meeting that would accomplish as much as what we could have done in thirty minutes in the absence of ministerial staff. When you fill a room with ministers, you're going to have a lot of rabbit trail conversations and storytelling. You also had a variety of strong personalities to deal with.

One person would facilitate the planning and call out a date to see if anybody had something to add to the calendar. We would proceed through the calendar one day at a time, plodding our way slowly through each month. With about twenty people at these meetings, they could bog down easily. Our lead pastor had monthly meetings with each individual pastor, and we would take the time to confirm each of those on the general church calendar. We also included all staff vacations or travel dates. I thought we were there to schedule events as a ministry and felt the business side of a calendar could easily be done via forms and emails. By the time we made it through a few weeks of details, people were getting visibly frayed around the edges, myself included. It wasn't uncommon to hear bickering over a vehicle that two different ministries needed for the same date. Each ministry had its own agenda and schedule without any united purpose or vision.

I thrive on efficiency and quick, basic details. I don't need the story behind the story. When you're recalling an event, I don't care if it was a Tuesday or a Wednesday. Our pastor was a storyteller, and he loved a captive audience. By captive, I mean, he was our boss. These meetings would drain the life from me. This was not what I imagined. What was the grand plan? Where was the idea that we are one family? Wasn't it important to coordinate activities and share the information? How could somebody pray for the teens attending a retreat if they didn't know it was happening? Why couldn't we connect generations through shared activities? I wanted us to be one family, fully informed of all family activities so we could support and care for all members. I didn't want us to be divided into small groups, friendships, or Bible study classes.

I am not a fan of children. To be honest, they kind of freak me out the way they look at you expectantly, and I can't understand what they say when they talk. Then there's the fact that they are walking germ factories with a mission to destroy my healthy cells. At least, that's how I see them. However, I love them, and I want to see them because they are a part of my church family. I want to pray for them, to know when they go to camp, and to know when one is being baptized or struggling.

I thought it was important to compare ministry schedules, so a worship volunteer meeting wasn't conflicting with a children's ministry team lunch. Perhaps even worse was when those two meetings would be back-to-back, or maybe a day apart. How were we caring for people if we were prioritizing individual ministry wants and needs over a life of balance for the church and volunteers? I watched so many volunteers burn out. Why weren't we putting their emotional, physical, and spiritual well-being as a top priority? Jesus modeled balance for a reason. At least, that's what I thought, and part of why these meetings frustrated me.

If you listened carefully, you would have heard the slow whine as my heart began to deflate like a balloon, the air steadily escaping through a small hole that was growing larger. Because the meetings would change when leadership transitioned, I continued to hang onto hope for the style of meeting I had envisioned. We were in transition again and I hoped the new pastor would bring something different, something I would align with and enjoy more. Was the next season different? Yes. Did it redeem my hopes? No. Neither did the several additional transitions that would follow. The best part of staff meetings was knowing I would be going to lunch afterward with Linda and Dana, fellow staffers who were great friends of mine, and we could talk through our shared frustrations.

Here's a newsflash for you. Church staff meetings can be as mundane as any other meeting you may have experienced. My job wasn't involved deeply in the weekly routine so I would often occupy myself with internal responses as noted below to pass the time while I waited for something that felt meaningful or was relevant to me.

Pastor: "I'm starting a new sermon series in two weeks, titled _____." *I could have filled in the blank for you with an example, but I wasn't paying much attention.*

Audio/Visual Guy: "Great. I already have the graphic for the sermon notes, slides, blah, blah, blah." *These were probably not his actual words, but I was still not focused on these minute details. This seemed like something to be discussed between them before updating the staff via email.*

Secretary: Our attendance Sunday was 329, which is up by fourteen from the week before, but down by 143 from last year. *Are the people in church growing closer to God? Why are people leaving?*

Audio/Visual Guy again: "I have Joe scheduled to do the announcements, but only these three, so it doesn't take too long. We're decreasing the bulletin count by thirty and collecting them for recycling. *Don't we want our bulletins to be important enough that people want to take them home and refer to the information during the week? Am I the only one who thinks like this?*

Facility Manager: "We need to set up four tables in the lobby tomorrow. We're cleaning the gutters this week. Oh, and they're striping the parking lot next Monday, so you'll need to park on the other side of the building." *This is not important and is wasting my time. We don't all need to know how many tables your team is setting up for an outside event in our building. Do you all need to know what projects I'm working on tomorrow? This could have been said in an email.*

Someone else from staff: "Are we still dumping out the unused communion crackers or repacking it to use again next week?" *WHAT? BACK THAT UP! Did you just say we are serving USED communion crackers that have been breathed on and perhaps coughed over by people, maybe even sick people?*

Yes, after enough bouts with bronchitis or pneumonia you are hyper-aware and sensitive to things like this. Not to mention that the membership was quite heavy on the senior citizen side, an age when health can be frail. But seriously, do we care so much about the pennies saved that we put our people at risk? Where is the love in that? I often imagined myself jumping on the conference room table, asking that very question. That's usually when I would have a slight smile on my face and my favorite co-worker, Linda, would know I was up to something in my imagination. We had to stop making eye contact during staff meetings for fear we would laugh. Dana had already moved on to another job, and the two of us missed having her at the meetings.

I wish I had counted how many times we talked about the policies that seemed to change consistently and yet would never be fully implemented. If Heaven had an admittance test, I imagine that is one of the questions for all former church employees. I can picture it now, with the little bubble circles listed for your answer options.

Question 1. How many weeks can a poster be on the windows to promote an event?

Question 2. How many announcements can we have on Sundays?

Question 3. Are food and beverages allowed in the Sanctuary?

Question 4. When a ministry reserves a room, do they need to empty the garbage?

This wasn't what I had hoped for. Quite frankly, I was disappointed, frustrated, and bored. I didn't care if red punch was allowed at events; I cared about people wanting to attend our events. Let the people have red punch! I can almost guarantee you red punch is allowed in Heaven. For me, the church is the world's living room, and it should look lived in. Love the people. You can clean the carpets!

I remember several times when people needed help or were facing surgery, crisis, job loss, or maybe even had a death in the family. We offered Sunday and Wednesday Bible classes, as well as small groups people could join for a more casual study format. These would meet on various days of the week to study, fellowship, and build community together. Our practice was to let the leader of a small group know when someone in their group had a need so they could connect and care for them. That's not a bad care structure. I didn't really have a problem with that until we had somebody who wasn't in a small group.

Without exception, the conversation would turn from the person in need to the fact that everybody should be in a small group and then rabbit trail off down that path, leaving the person, and their need, in the dust. *Wait. What? Did that just happen? Did we really ignore the opportunity to serve somebody? Are we punishing them for not being part of a small group? I must have missed that part in the Bible when it says to love others unless they aren't part of the right program at your church.* One of my favorite co-workers, Jeffrey, shared the same frustrations and would step in and ask, "Are we going to help them since they aren't in a small group or punish them for not being in one?" I was always so proud of him for the way he lived out his faith. He was a great example of loving people.

A church staff meeting is just that, a staff meeting. I'm sorry to disappoint you if you also expected more. That discouragement began to chip away at my belief that the church would make a difference in our community. If a process or program became more important than a person, I didn't hold out hope that our love would show through.

The God I knew wouldn't be thrilled with what I saw in staff meetings. I think it might have even brought Him sorrow at times. I thought church was about serving people, teaching them, coming alongside, and helping people develop their spiritual growth while deepening their relationship with God. I thought it was about loving them and I thought it was about reaching out to the community beyond our walls and serving them. We seemed to be more concerned with the comfort of the people already in our congregation. Notice I said their comfort, not even their growth. If we were going to focus only inwardly, at least we could strengthen the faith and relationships they had with God.

It confused and disappointed me to hear so much conversation about logistics and programs, and so little about people and God. Where was prayer? Under some leadership, decisions were made based on fear, or what man could do instead of what God could do. I felt prayer should have been an automatic response far more often. I was sad to see we didn't always have faith, prayer, and trusting God modeled for us as the clear first steps. It was heartbreaking. How sad that time and time again, prayer was a last resort after trying to handle things with human capabilities. Why wasn't the first step to trust God and see what His guidance might be? This played out repeatedly for years.

It wasn't always like that. There were times a situation would come up and we would stop to pray about it. Maybe it was about an individual's need, a situation within the church, or a decision needing to be made. Jeffrey would often lightheartedly toss out the phrase, "Prayer? Has it come to that?" It made for a smile at the time and a gentle reminder that prayer is so important and should always be a first consideration. Sadly, we don't get to hear those words now as he is busy celebrating, singing, and dancing in God's presence. Jeffrey's words will always remind a lot of folks of the beauty of prayer.

After we plodded our way through the agenda, discussion would open for any additional new business we may not have covered. On occasion, the worship pastor would ask, "Should we have patriotic songs and the flag for Memorial Day?" There would be a few nods in agreement before we'd quickly move on.

Attendance numbers mattered to the lead pastor so during camp season, it wasn't uncommon to hear him inquire, "How many people were away at youth camp? Did we add them to the count for Sunday?"

After the general discussion completed, we'd go one-by-one around the table to ask each person if they had anything they wanted to bring up. Most people did not, but there were a few that seemed to always have something they were anxious to talk about. Sometimes it was something personal about what was happening in their life, or a prayer request, and those were precious moments. Usually, it was more time spent on things that didn't need to be addressed in a group of all staff.

The lead pastor would inquire with the bookkeeper. "Nothing, except timesheets are due."

Next was the office manager. "Nope, we've covered everything I had." *Whew! We were moving right along. Maybe we'd get done early this time and could find a good parking spot at lunch.*

One by one, he would call people out around the table to give them an opportunity to speak up. "I'm good." "Nope." "I'm going to be out of the office tomorrow on vacation." *Yes, we were making substantial progress.*

Does God Attend Staff Meetings?

Then I heard it, like the brakes on a semi-truck screeching on a downhill grade. "Well..." This long, drawn-out word may have been followed with a long list of all activities from a particular ministry. Sometimes it was a list of questions someone had about a previous discussion, now that they had time to think about it more.

One or two more with nothing to discuss, my optimism was growing and then it came crashing down as the maintenance staff brought up their repeated concern about people throwing their coffee cups into the trash bags without emptying the liquid first. I don't recall that I've ever been to a place that didn't allow us to throw away garbage and this topic really frustrated me. If we don't want liquid in the garbage bags, stop serving coffee. If you want to serve coffee, buy thicker garbage bags. It was simple for me, but nobody could ever seem to settle it and I was tired of it taking time regularly.

There was one topic that consistently pushed my buttons and nearly had me walking out of meetings and out the door for good. Funerals. When there was a memorial service, discussions turned to creating a slideshow, PowerPoint, or printed program and I knew I was going to hear, "We're not a funeral home." Additionally, it was common to hear, "It can't be on a Saturday, that's my day off." Sometimes, I even heard other staff say, "It can't be on a Saturday, it's too hard to set up for church afterward." I am proud of myself for never losing it and going off on these comments. I'm SURE the person didn't mean to die on the wrong day. I'm SURE we wouldn't want to make this time any easier for the grieving family and friends, or to show compassion or love to them. You're right, we are NOT a funeral home. WE ARE THE CHURCH!!!!!!!! OK, so much for not ever losing it, but I feel better now.

We had connection cards in our bulletin so people could update their contact information. This is also where they would write any comments or prayer requests. If they had any ministry interests or questions about the church, they could check those boxes as well. They might have had a broken back and needed help with errands, or maybe they had a Bible question. Whatever it was, it provided an easy way to communicate with staff.

Often people were sharing a concern, complaint, or question about church and didn't feel comfortable to sign their name. I've always had a heart for the type of people who aren't confident enough to confront or complain. I can be that way myself. Some in leadership would not value these, and it ached to know those voices would not be heard. It was another clarifying moment that confirmed I probably didn't belong there.

I remember when an elderly member needed a fence repaired. We had a newly single mother needing lessons on home repair after her husband abruptly abandoned his family. My heart crumbled when I heard leadership ask, "How is that our problem?" I know God was grieved. When one of the family needs help, it IS our problem, and it should be our joyous responsibility to serve them if we can. I'm not trying to describe myself as the only one who felt this way. I know for a fact several people felt the same way because they told me.

I lost my first bit of enthusiasm and confidence in church due to staff meetings. The things I experienced forced me to question if my purpose really included working at a church. I yearned for more. I wanted to see lives changed and God honored. I wanted to see people serving each other without having to sign up for a program to do so. I feared we were making people's faith dependent upon the church and not God.

Maybe I was naïve, but I believed working at a church would be the best job anybody could hope for, and I could help change lives by working there. Based on what I was experiencing, I was starting to question the purpose and function of the church. I no longer wanted to be there on Sundays. In fact, you could say being on staff led me a great distance down the path toward the conclusion that I hated church. I knew with certainty I no longer looked forward to staff meetings.

I reconnected with Doug C., who had been an area youth minister when I was a teenager. In those days we would join with other youth groups for larger multi-congregational youth rally events. This happened often, which allowed for numerous friendships across the state, many that are still in place decades later. Recently, I struggled to understand why I felt so unsettled and I began searching for people who remembered what I was like as a teenager. Even though our only contact in the last thirty-five years was through social media, Doug came to mind. After a couple of brief emails, he set up a time for us to talk. I positioned myself in the most tranquil room of my home, where I could see outside to the trees while kicking back on my chaise. This was my room for the important stuff, away from the busyness of real life happening on my street. In other words, a place where I couldn't hear my dog barking at any of his enemies; the mail carrier, the blade of grass that twitched in the breeze, or the scary attack fly on the next block over.

I gathered a notebook, pen, and a bottle of water before settling in. We spoke for a few hours and it felt like no time had passed. We filled in the gaps that spanned three decades. As he recalled the teenage version of me, he told me, "You were never content to simply do something without knowing why." Instead, I felt there should be a purpose behind our actions, and I always needed a larger reason why. He also mentioned that I thought there was more to faith than only going to church. That seemed to explain a lot of my journey and discontent. His last revelation was a surprise to me, and I took it as a compliment. He described me by saying, "You would always ask the bigger questions, questions most people don't ask, adults included."

This was one of those pivotal moments in my journey, although he didn't know it. I suddenly had the reason behind so much of my staff meeting frustrations. Indeed, I was NOT content to do things without knowing it served a larger God-driven purpose. I spent years not realizing this was one of the ways God designed me to specifically be able to live for Him. We are all called into a life that embraces the special design God wove into us. If you don't know and understand your uniqueness, I hope and pray you will choose to search that out. I allowed the opinions of others to influence the way I interpreted the value of my individuality. It's easy for us to do that. Maybe we have discarded or diminished it ourselves based on our own expectations. Please find people who know you and will help you discover who God made you to be. Don't let the actions, or inactions of others hold you back from being 100% you. I had forgotten who I was, and I became an emptier version while on staff. I was a mere shell of who I was meant to be.

I eventually allowed the actions of others in leadership to have a negative influence on how I viewed church. A church staff meeting can be all about church logistics or it can lean more toward integrating God's vision into what church looks like. I can now look back with a heart of gratitude because while those kinds of things eventually drove me away from church, it helped to drive me straight into the arms of God. Staff meetings left me wanting more, and I finally discovered it was God my soul had been craving.

Chapter 8
DO I HAVE TO GO TO CHURCH?

CHURCH. WORSHIP. THE ASSEMBLY. SERVICES. It didn't matter what you called it, I hated going. There, I said it. Wow, confession really is good for the soul. Maybe James was onto something when he suggested confessing our sins in James chapter five. It is common for people working traditional weekday schedules to feel a dread on Sundays as they anticipate Monday coming. Well, that was me on Saturday night, anticipating with dread, the arrival of Sunday morning. I frequently allowed it to steal my Saturday. I didn't want to get up and I had no drive to do anything fun. All I could see was Sunday looming over me. I had never dreaded Sundays prior to being on staff. I think we can agree that the church is the people, not the building. But when you are in that building five to six days a week, it does remove a little of the sense that it is a special place.

Any number of things could be the catalyst for this near-weekly sense of dread. Our staff changed frequently, and this often affected how I viewed Sundays. There were times when I found the music lethargic and uninspiring. I didn't often relate to the sermon. I was frustrated by the typos on the song slides and I occupied myself making notes to send to the ministry leader to have them fixed. I didn't like the miniature sermon before communion. I thought putting out a donation box for the donuts was tacky. Really? How is that hospitable and welcoming?

At the top of my "Things I Loathe About Sundays" list was the everybody stand and shake hands welcome time introverts feared. I secretly came to refer to this as the dreaded meet and greet. In my opinion, being told to do something renders it disingenuous. If I'm going to shake someone's hand and say hello, I'm going to mean it and I want them to as well. As an introvert, I also suspected this was a detriment to a lot of guests and all other introverts. For me, it was always followed by a quick run to the bathroom to wash my hands. More times than not, I would run into others doing the same thing.

I was tired of regimented programming. We had one pastor who would use a stopwatch to time things down to the minute and copy it exactly for the second service, word for word. He was known to talk to the worship leader after the first service to request things speed up or even to cut a line from a song. I'm told by other staff who were working at both services he never shortened his sermon if the first service was a few minutes long.

I wanted to see what would happen if we stepped aside and allowed God to run things. What if we prayed for the congregation and asked God to speak into the direction we took for services? I know we needed plans, but I thought we should allow for wiggle room in case God wanted to do something. I didn't see God at the center of our church services, being the purpose behind every component on Sundays. I was growing bitter and angry, to the point I looked for excusable reasons to not be at church.

While I felt this so deeply at my home congregation, it wasn't exclusive to them. I have always had connections with other churches and often visited to learn about innovations we might adopt. Many reflected God well, while others seemed to be more self-focused. I found myself wondering if God was pleased with what modern society had done to His church. Is this what He intended for our time together? Is there a missing book of the Bible that says a church worship service must have one song, announcements, two shorter songs, prayer, one song, communion, two songs, sermon, invitation, and one more song before dismissal back to our homes? I suspect that many churches have lost sight of their purpose and have become too focused on the programming aspect of a "successful church service" experience.

I don't believe Church is about the count of people in attendance. Nor is it about the right number of announcements, or which ones were worthy of being listed. I'm sure the format of the bulletin isn't relevant either. I can't believe God cares if someone spills coffee on the floor of the Sanctuary. I honestly think God might take delight with the sprinkles on a donut in the lobby. Yes, there were rules about what kinds of donuts could be served. No sprinkles because they could be messy, especially with children there. Now, I understand there's a side to being a good steward and that includes the building. I had to wonder; maybe God was more concerned with that kid feeling welcomed in the church building than a few sprinkles on the floor. We know Jesus delighted in children. Children delight in sprinkles. I'm guessing God does, too!

I believe church services are about showing Christ's love and acceptance, so nobody leaves feeling alone. It means being aware of people and truly seeing them so we know if there is a need we can help with or a hurt we can pray about. We should be showing the way to God and salvation. It is about sharing the burdens of others. It is about encouraging one another, feeding one another, and loving one another. It is about learning from God's word, one of the best ways we can get to know Him.

Churches have far fewer second-time visitors than first-time visitors. Do we ever stop to ask ourselves why? Is it possible they showed up the first time looking for God but couldn't find Him? It sounds harsh, but are we brave enough to consider this? We've all heard people say nobody talked to them and they felt like they weren't welcome. It's difficult to be new, and we should strive to be welcoming to all. Sundays are for church, not for social exclusion. God asked us; no, he COMMANDED us, to love one another. That doesn't mean some of the people. We should keep our heads up and look for people who need us. They are there every week, and most won't ask for help.

One day I was sitting in my church office when Jason, a Christian police officer friend of mine stopped by to check in on me. He had a heart for our church because we were in the same community where he served as a School Resource Officer. My husband and I had recently visited his congregation when he filled in to preach. I told him how much we enjoyed the services there, the music, and the warm welcome. I shared some of the most impactful moments from his sermon and thanked him for the invitation to visit. It had been a refreshing church visit. He knew how we felt about our own church services.

He then turned the focus of the conversation from our visit to his church and nonchalantly asked, "What do you think of the music here?" I looked away. It isn't necessary to be the "polite, church-leadership-supporting, they might be watching me for an example, must be professional" kind of friend. When he asked questions, he wanted the genuine answers I would usually gloss over for others. Jason was someone I could confide in and share with when discouraged. He was a great encouragement to my own spiritual growth, and I could trust him completely to share my burdens.

It surprised me to realize I was nervous to respond. I wasn't sure why. Maybe I was afraid to be openly truthful about it. My reply was simple and honest. "If I were attending here for the first time, I wouldn't come back." I've experienced many better options and I've experienced worse. It's just that our current music didn't resonate with me. I didn't connect to God during the musical worship time, no matter how hard I tried to. Instead, I would find myself feeling sad and empty, while longing for more. I love worship music, but often found myself grumbling about what it could be and comparing it to past styles I enjoyed and appreciated.

As I sat there waiting for a judgment that would never come, I heard him ask, "What do you think about the preaching?" Once again, I shifted my focus to the bookcase, or the floor, I can't remember which. I finally made eye contact with him and took a deep breath. "I don't connect, I don't retain much, and I usually wait for it to be over each week. The truth is, I often give up and resort to making grocery lists during the sermon."

Then came his third and most challenging question. Jason looked me in the eye and gently asked, "Is it competent and biblical?" I felt broken and convicted inside, as I mumbled out a quiet, "Yes." I wanted to be nothing but truthful and open with him. Remember, he was in uniform. Even though he was a friend, there's an extra something about trying to bluff an answer to a man in a police uniform.

The problem wasn't the music. The problem wasn't the sermon. Nor was it the typos, the meet and greet, or the bulletin. The problem was me. I tend to find God deeper in ways that are not reflected in a Sunday worship time.

One pastor we had was a watchdog on attendance. It became such an obligation to punch in each week that it grew to have absolutely nothing to do with God. I wasn't one of the sheep there, I was merely a number needing to be counted so things would reflect well on him.

I was disappointed with church. I resented having to be there. Like the strongest of weeds, the roots of bitterness strengthened as they grew deeper.

I tried to appreciate Sunday worship services while working there, but it became increasingly more difficult. It was an easy thing for me to switch gears and find that comfort zone of selfishness and resentment. I wanted the freedom afforded to others. I wanted the option to go spend time with God the way I enjoyed.

I started to think if consistent attendance was more important to them than a genuine connection to God and spiritual growth, then they should pay us for Sundays. I didn't like being told how to worship God to fit their agenda. At least, that's how I explained it to my friends.

There is a wonderful book, *Sacred Pathways: Nine Ways to Connect with God* by Gary Thomas which helped me understand why this was so difficult for me. When I read this book, it opened my eyes to see why I didn't connect deeply with God through church services, sermons, or quiet times.

I have two main pathways I use to find God. My strongest is through nature, or creation. My second one uses my senses, especially music and artistic creativity. It isn't permission to ignore the other pathways, but it was a bright light shining on why I felt different. I finally had permission to worship in the manner that felt right to me. But due to my job, I was stuck attending church by a leadership that would never understand that there are other pathways to God.

Do I Have to Go to Church?

I wanted to be in nature or rocking out to some high-powered music somewhere. Or better yet, rocking out to rhythm-filled worship music while driving through nature! Oh, how I longed to be driving through the countryside taking scenic pictures, stopping to listen to the waterfalls or the rushing rivers. I preferred to pause in the still silence of open fields and back, unpopulated roads to sit quietly in God's presence. Sometimes I dreamed of painting in my studio. There were even times I wanted to be reading the Bible in my special tropical-themed "woman cave" at home, surrounded by objects that inspire me or remind me of who God created me to be. I enjoyed being with friends and talking about how God was working around us. Any of these would have helped me develop a closer relationship with God than sitting in church, especially when I was often griping about having to be there.

I didn't want to occupy a pew at church on Sundays, reciting over and over in my head the verse in Hebrews 10:25, where we are told not to forsake the assembly, as is the practice of some. I didn't want to be trapped into mandatory attendance because the pastor was concerned about what people would think if a staff member wasn't there every Sunday. I wanted to be with God, and I preferred to hang out with Him at different times and in different places. Church was not a necessary event in my life and was diminishing my relationship with God and my fellow Christians.

After years of this weekly battle, I sat there scanning the audience when it suddenly hit me. This is my church family! Like them or not, know them all or not, this is the family I chose to be a part of. I had been through a lot of traumatic events at this congregation, including a church split. I've often heard it said that we don't choose our family. You will usually hear this in the context of a dysfunctional family or relatives who do not like each other. But, by staying at this church, I had chosen this as my family.

To me, family meant people who loved you, people who would help you if there was something that happened. Family was a group of people at the top of the guest list, the people that mattered most, even if you liked some of them a little less than others. With that being said, I realized that while this was technically my church family, they didn't feel like a group of people that cared about me and my well-being. Certainly not to the depth I had known family to be in the past, at other churches.

As I reflected on our experiences there, the more my own desires surfaced instead of God's. I found myself caring less and less about being a part of that church family. My husband was already disconnected from there. I was emotionally disconnected as well. Unfortunately, I was still tethered due to my employment. It had once been a home for us, and a family where we loved, and were loved. Time had broken that apart. This was no longer the place we had once chosen to call home.

Growing up, I had a remarkable church home until it split. Even though I have not seen or heard the names of most of them for almost four decades, my heart swells with joy when I think of them. So many of the memories centered around serving together and fellowship, a lot of fellowship. The people came together to care for and comfort everyone there because we were all family. I was missing that in this current church, due to so many transitions.

While I grew up in the Church of Christ, I have since proclaimed I would never return. A minister friend of mine, Rick, made me look him in the eyes as he said, "Never say never," and then grinned. I shook it off. I do have a new church home that is not a Church of Christ, and I feel like I'm settling in nicely. But roots run deep, and I continue to meet weekly with a small group that is a part of Metro Church of Christ, where my friend Rick serves. I have even visited their church services from time to time. It feels like a visit home. Perhaps I never should have said, "Never."

One of the most beautiful and remarkable things I've ever witnessed is the way the Church of Christ models family. It is one thing I have come to appreciate deeply. The first time Tracy and I visited Metro was to hear Rick speak. We entered the building as outsiders, looking only to visit once to hear an old friend preach. We slid into a pew near the back of the auditorium just after services began so we could avoid conversations. We are both introverts. We huddled close, believing we were invisible during the meet and greet. With our heads down, reading the bulletin repeatedly and not making eye contact with others, we thought we could go unnoticed. That only lasted a few minutes before half a dozen people walking up and down the aisle stopped to shake our hands and introduce themselves. Not only did they introduce themselves, but they asked questions about who we were and how we came to be at Metro that day.

When services ended, we made a quick beeline for the exit door where we were stopped by the older gentleman who had first greeted us as he called out, "We'll go to lunch next time you're here." We entered as strangers, we left as family. I knew deep inside that they loved us unconditionally simply because we were brothers and sisters in Christ. They would have stepped in to help if we needed anything, even though we had just met. I couldn't have known that three years later, a group of men would come install handrails to help me recover from cancer surgery. It was a beautiful example of love, and I am grateful this level of brotherly love is in my foundation of faith. I hope I never lose respect for that and pray I can model it wherever I am.

Sadly, sometimes a church is simply a group of people who attend services together. Friendships may form naturally within the mix of people. Churches will either draw you to God or draw you to programs, leaving you perplexed and wondering where God was. If you pay attention, you can see the underlying current that leadership has created, defining who they are and what their purpose is. Please be sure you find a church that draws you to God and folds you in as family. These are the people who understand God's plan and will hold you up when you need it. Don't forget that you are also a child of God and family to them as well, so you have a responsibility to them.

Church leadership gets a lot of feedback about weekend services. It's mostly negative. I'd encourage you to compliment them and show your appreciation. They need to hear that.

One of the most common complaints we heard was about the volume or style of the music. This is true for most churches. It's become culturally popular, and I have experienced this, to hear church leaders respond with the statement, "It's not about personal preferences." Maybe it's not. When attendance starts to decline, those are the same pastors who are quick to say, "Attendance numbers don't matter." Hmmm . . .

I would argue it might be about the music, the sermon, or the attendance drop. Maybe there is a spiritual battle or crisis happening for those people. Maybe it should be about noticing when someone has been gone for months. I believe the spiritual health of the church is what matters most. However, when numbers decline, it may be worth asking the hard questions to discover why. A congregation full of people not connecting with God won't be serving Him or inviting people to meet Him at church.

I believe every attendee has a voice deserving to be heard and offers a different perspective leadership may not have. We are there to serve and if we don't even know the people we are serving, something is wrong. Those little white connection cards from the pews were important to me. I don't care if it was anonymous or not, it mattered to somebody enough to share and should be weighed. I've often wondered how many people each voice represented. According to Lee Resource, every complaint represents twenty-six other people who have remained silent. If our sermons are not connecting people to God, maybe we need to listen and prayerfully consider changes. If you are a leader reading this, please look at why people leave or stay on the fringe.

Do I Have to Go to Church?

Yes, many people church-hop because of personal preferences. That may not be the best approach for a few reasons, and I'm going to be candid here; you are likely not seeking God, but your own pleasures. In addition, you aren't apt to build that bond as a church family to serve and to serve with. I think it may honor God to leave a church if we don't see God's love being lived out well. We should be prayerful and cautious, to be sure we are not using our preferences as our guide.

If you are pointing out something that may hinder the ability to reach the lost, and you are not heard, leaving might be the right thing to do. If you are following God, I believe He will direct you to the local congregation where He wants you to be. Church attendance should be an act that comes from loving God wholeheartedly and obeying His desires for us. It should never stem from the burden of obligation. I also believe the most important relationship is the one with God. Eventually, I'm certain He will lead you to attend church. I'm okay if it's not every week. Please don't tell anybody I said that! But, seriously, I believe sometimes the priority of loving God may look like a weekend with your spouse, a day painting, or a road trip.

I allowed the frustrations with the job and the people at church to chip away at my faith repeatedly until being at church became one of the biggest obstacles to my faith.

I am not the only person this has happened to, and I hope it has not happened to you, and never will. I let the weariness, disappointments, and bitterness destroy my Sunday time with God. It became a chore worse than any I could have imagined, usually taking a day or two to recover from emotionally. I let people have too much input on my Christian walk and I allowed them to stand between me and God.

Like children, it's time to find those sprinkles. Kids may put sprinkles on sundaes, but I think it's high time we find those sprinkles of joy that can come on Sundays!

Chapter 9
WHAT'S IT GOING TO TAKE?

THERE WERE TWO STAFF EVENTS that were the highlight of each year. While different from each other, they both helped with the renewal and restoration of staff. For many years there was an annual winter staff and elders retreat at the beach. The focus was on prayer, planning, reflection, and ministry. Spouses were invited and there were some years when ministry team leaders were also included. The Global Leadership Summit (GLS) every August focused on leadership training.

Many of the early staff retreats brought us closer together through the shared experience of worship and prayer. Before attending my first one, I feared it would be a formal setting and each person would be required to pray. I wasn't comfortable praying aloud and wasn't looking forward to the event. It turned out that they were casual, relaxed, and not the least bit intimidating.

When the budget tightened, the GLS attendance was eliminated. This was a crushing blow for me personally. In 2007, my boss included me as part of the leadership team for our ministry area and asked me to attend my first GLS. This annual event is where I was exposed to leadership development and personal assessments. My life continues to be impacted by what I learned at the GLS events through the years. They were so life-altering, I continued to attend on my own. I gained a deeper understanding of my strengths, my personality tendencies, my leadership traits, and my expectations of leaders around me.

My boss, Kurt, had been leading our ministry team through personal assessment and development, but the GLS speakers gave us more tools and training to incorporate. It was a time of significant growth and our specific ministry team was unified and bonded. Personal development became a priority for me and a way of life that continues to serve me well. I viewed it as essential to keep our church moving forward and it was the only coaching or training provided to our staff to fuel growth within our leaders.

The first year of the budget cuts, we did a combined event, with our pastor showing a few of the leadership videos on DVD at the staff prayer retreat. It was good information, but it felt lifeless. Linda, the office manager friend of mine, felt the same way. We both missed the connections and transparent conversations that came when attending the event together. We vowed we would pay our own way if the church budget wasn't able to cover us because we both craved the training and growth.

Senior leadership transitioned once more, and we spent a couple of years without a lead pastor. I pitched the idea of combining the prayer meeting and the leadership conference training. I received approval from the elders, and Linda and I presented the training to the group for a couple of years.

One year I scheduled a session about innovation. Our speaker used the analogy of the high jump, and how it developed from the scissor kick to the Fosbury Flop. The training session was powerful, showing how vital innovation is, whether it be in business, church, or personal development. If you want to remain relevant, it is essential to innovate.

He used the high jump as his example and quoted the heights reached using the original method and the traditional scissor kick. Then he introduced us to the history of the Fosbury Flop and how the heights attained far exceeded any other method. From what I could find in a quick internet search, it looks like the last time the men's world record was set using the scissor kick was 1912. Let that sink in. 1912. Remember this number.

I led our group through a general discussion. We identified those we felt had an innovative mindset and spent some time talking about things we needed to change if we wanted the church to reach and serve our neighborhood effectively. We were seated at long tables formed into a square, filling the meeting room, so we could see each other as we talked. I happened to be seated parallel to one of our elders when he spoke up and voiced the question, "What's wrong with the scissor kick?"

I felt as if someone had punched me in the gut and knocked the wind out of me. I did my best not to let my facial expression reflect my thoughts. I found myself grateful for the five people sitting between us, blocking me from his view. A quick glance around the room told me 90% of the staff but only one of the elders wanted to respond with, "Everything!" I tried to imagine a situation where it made sense not to consider new approaches, when the old ones clearly were no longer working. If you were going to compete in the Olympics today, would you attempt the high jump with the scissor kick when your competition is reaching soaring heights using the innovative technique? I didn't have the courage to speak up and believed there wasn't any hope left. I saw no reason to speak my response aloud. Instead, I fought to keep the tears from cresting over my eyelids and commented only in my mind. What was my internal response to his question about the scissor kick? "I repeat, 1912."

It's as if the long red velvet curtains parted and the stage light revealed a truth I had not accepted before. We were always going to be stuck in the old ways. I also saw the chasm between the staff and elders widen. I knew it existed, but I hoped it would merge by spending time growing together. The leadership was not all on the same page. I wanted desperately to align with the elders, but that likelihood was growing slim. This was never going to get better. This was not going to be the kind of effective and efficient place I wanted to be a part of. My calling to this job was being lifted as it began transitioning into a routine job, a job I could choose to walk away from.

I remember sitting next to one of our elders during another session when the topic turned to the current rift in the church. We were having an issue with someone being divisive and we were still dealing with some hurt people from the church split. We had had several staffing transitions in recent years; some of them had gone poorly, leaving hurt and destruction in their wake. All of us were exhausted from years of this turmoil. We were deeply hurt ourselves, while busily caring for others. Wounded people were trying to figure out how to handle the current crisis.

The discussion surged, sometimes from a place of anger but often from a place of mercy. In the end, there was a plan with two clear directions to take and many ideas to implement. The primary direction focused on how best to grow the faith of those who remained in the church, and how to care for and encourage them. The other half of the plan was created with specific steps listed to stop the spread of lies from the disgruntled people. There was a church announcement scheduled to clarify the situation to the congregation. During the discussion, one elder I highly respected, leaned over to me and said what a few of us were thinking, "It sure seems like something we should pray about." The idea that prayer was not the first step revealed a bigger gap than I expected to see between where I wanted to be and where I was. If I had been keeping a pros and cons list about staying in my job, this would have added one more tally to the con side of staying.

After doing some leadership training at these retreats for at least two years, I scheduled one session as a challenge and review of the previous retreat. I had one goal in mind, to take an honest look at the purpose and effectiveness of the time we spent together each year. I had prepared a list of what we covered the prior year, including speakers, topics, key points, and a few of my notes from our group discussion.

I planned to ask them for volunteers to share how their lives had been changed from anything they learned.

Were they scheduling meetings with their teams differently? Had they begun any new habits? I wanted to know what they incorporated from the trainings. I expected it would be completely silent, yet foolishly hoped for one or two comments from the entire group. It was my belief that our leadership didn't want to grow or didn't believe it was necessary. I wanted to use this exercise to suggest we drop this part of the retreat. The other option was to commit to a culture of development. I wasn't holding my breath for that commitment.

I didn't get the chance to conduct that session. On the break before, a side conversation came up about a ministry idea one of the staff spouses had. Danny was there, with his wife Hannah, who was our Director of Children's Ministry. They both have a passion for fishing, but Danny's enthusiasm for it is remarkable. He wanted to start a fishing ministry. This would incorporate all ages and genders, allowing for a lot of relationships to be established while having fun.

It was a great idea, an innovative one, and I had no problem being fluid with our schedule. After all, listening to the needs and passions of our congregation is at the foundation of why we're here to serve. One of the elders asked if we could take a few more minutes to talk about the idea. I was excited. This was innovation, and they were welcoming it. Instead of holding us accountable to following through, we spent the entire session making plans for this new ministry.

Nothing ever happened. There never was a fishing ministry developed. I was not surprised. Oddly enough, that interruption gave me the answer I anticipated from the originally planned segment. Perhaps another tally mark on the con side of things again.

This was the same event I mentioned previously, where we had a difficult and divisive situation and prayer was not what our leaders turned to first. That was a huge and bitter disappointment. The very thing that set us apart from a business, our faith, was not having any noticeable impact on our actions.

After hearing so much about the qualities of influential leaders and watching the emphasis on the importance of leaders continuing to grow and learn, it was disheartening to see our leaders not place a value on these things. Only Linda and I continued to attend the annual GLS conference. We tried to share what we learned with some of our co-workers, but it fell on deaf ears. Instead, we encouraged each other and continued to grow so we could make an impact in other circles of influence. Sometimes leadership doesn't lead. The truth is, nobody else is responsible for our growth and maturity. It's wonderful when you have a leadership you align with, but we can still grow without that in place. I've worked for outstanding leaders people respect and want to follow. I've also worked for bosses who are there only to manage their staff, enjoy having power, and bask in the accolades. There is a big difference between the two and it isn't worth the personal loss to work for a boss.

The question I had been asking myself for years, "How much longer can I stay here?" was entering my thoughts more often. My friend, and former co-worker, Dana and I were once talking through some of the trauma and transitions when she lovingly asked, "What's it going to take for you to leave?" We looked at each other and burst into laughter. It sounded like she was asking how to get rid of me. I had my answer, but I still clung to hope. I noticed another crack forming in the foundation of my faith. My trust in leadership was becoming shaky. Disappointment with leadership is particularly difficult to process.

Chapter 10
WHY DOES THIS HURT SO MUCH?

IN MY FIRST DRAFT, I CONSIDERED *Division, Invisibility, and Other Perks of a Church Job* as the title for this chapter. Then I realized there was one word that best encompassed everything I was feeling. Disappointment. I'm including the original title for reference as my humorous attempt to explain what was happening in my heart, and to my faith, the longer I stayed on staff. Disappointment with church is a heavy burden to carry. As a staff member, it was one that I carried mostly alone as an act of love and care for the people in that church.

Rightly, there is an expectation of absolute confidentiality placed on all church staff. Part of our purpose is to care for the members of the congregation. As such, we are aware of the many burdens people carry and the heartaches they endure. In any group that size, there are countless people suffering in silence through trauma, sin, doubts, or trials. It was truly a joy to share in the spiritual journey of so many people, but there is a cost to caring. It's a cost I'd like to believe all church employees happily pay. I suspect that isn't true.

It is not unusual for staff, and pastors especially, to not have an adequate support system. There are a handful of people to help carry their burdens. As Christians, we need to pray for church leadership on a regular basis. It is a wonderful, yet troublesome, role to have. It is an honor to love people so deeply. It is a joy to choose to protect them from your disappointments. But leaders cannot do it alone. They should not do it alone.

I was living in a divided world. You didn't have to search far to find a divisive topic, even beyond the usual triggers based on differences in views on politics, race, or religion. Society was dealing with Black Lives Matter vs. All Lives Matter. School provided options for public, private, or homeschooling and there were opinions to be found wherever you turned. Homelessness was prevalent, yet nobody could agree on the next steps or a remedy. The best way to care for our planet was up for debate, as was most any topic. Our world was certainly not united. The citizens of the *United* States of America couldn't agree on many things. Churches across the world absolutely were not unified, but I had hoped, naïvely, our local congregation could be.

Why Does This Hurt So Much?

For the most part, I welcome and embrace change. I get bored easily, and I'm wired to look for efficiency and innovation, which leads to a lot of change. I'm one of those who finds it exhilarating to rearrange furniture and not follow the conventional ideas. Currently, my dining table is in the living room window near the fireplace to provide a cozy space, much like you'd find at your neighborhood coffee house. Because I embrace breaking up the routine, it caught me off guard to see it upset people so easily.

Many churches make a lot of changes as they search for ways to be more effective or efficient. Our building capacity was nearly 1,000 with a main floor that held the majority of seats, and a balcony that wrapped around the entire curve accommodating several hundred. Sometimes we roped off sections of pews to concentrate folks into a smaller space when attendance was low. To my amazement, we had people remove the ropes because they wanted to sit in their usual rows. As attendance continued to decrease, we consolidated three services into two. We closed the balcony to draw people closer physically and had to listen to more complaints.

"We like to spread out."

"We like looking down at the stage."

"This is where we've sat for years."

Later we would combine our two services into one to keep the church family together and connected. Each change was greeted with complaints. The grumbling when we changed from pews to chairs still echoes in my head.

"The chairs aren't as comfortable as the pews."

"I miss the shelf on the pew to hold my Bible."

"Why did we spend money to do this?"

"What was wrong with the old way?"

Our staff and elders were divided about allowing beverages into the sanctuary. "We don't sing enough hymns" warred against "we sing too many." The sound was either too loud or too soft, as were the drums. When communion time was moved from before the sermon to after, or to the very end of services, we heard about it. The first time we changed up that routine, you could have heard a pin drop, even on the carpeted floor. Sitting about five rows from the front, dead center, was a white-haired senior lady who had been attending for decades. As the pastor took the stage to begin preaching, she stood up quickly to face him. With a resolve you could see set in her shoulders, she firmly asked, "Why haven't we taken communion?" The pastor stopped speaking, and flustered, stammered out a slow, "I assure you we did not forget communion. Just this one time, we thought it would have more meaning at the end of the sermon."

WHY DOES THIS HURT SO MUCH?

It was disheartening to hear so much negativity over what I felt were frivolous and minute details. Each time people complained about the order of service, the types of songs, how big the bulletin was, or what we sat on, the focus was taken off God and placed on individuals. I certainly had my own preferences as well. We all do. I wasn't expecting to see how often a group of people could prioritize their own wants over the purpose of the church. It seemed we had become a private club instead of God's light shining outward.

I had not viewed congregational changes from a staff perspective before, and I wasn't prepared for the complaints based solely on personal dissatisfaction. We certainly had our hands full when significant changes came like worship music styles or a new pastor.

As if there wasn't enough emotional division, I found it surprising to see such a focus on physical division. Most of our church activities were broken into the ministry of small groups or Bible classes. I came from a background of Sunday morning Bible study classes for all ages, followed by church services that included every age group. We returned Sunday night for a second church service. Wednesday nights included time together in worship and prayer before we split out into classes. Once a month it was a night of congregational singing instead. There were so many opportunities for community-building, and the sense of family to develop. We were able to spend time building relationships with the entire church family and we never doubted that everybody had our back and we had theirs.

Now I was part of a church that seemed to be divided most of the time. Instead of one church family, it felt like multiple little churches sharing one building. Sundays had the Bible classes I was familiar with for most of my years there. Then we met for church services, but it didn't include children. The kids had their own worship time and lesson in another part of the building. Teenagers were sometimes there, but often not, depending on what program was in place.

We didn't meet for services on Sunday nights. Instead, people were divided out again, into the small groups that met in homes. Wednesday nights were church services for a few years. We all met in the Sanctuary for singing, prayer, Bible reading, and a quick lesson together. This kept us all in one place, and we had time to meet people and talk after church. It was the highlight of my week, and a nice bridge to get from one Sunday to the next. Then the program changed and became another time for divided activities, either small groups or classes.

I wanted to be a church together and meet people, find connections, and know what my community looked like. Instead, we were forced into smaller groups where people may or may not have connected with the other participants. Gone were the spur-of-the-moment dinners or ice cream outings after church I treasured from my childhood. No more all-church potlucks. Later came multiple services, even growing to three for a while. It was impossible to know my church family, as I would not meet many of them. This was new for me and left me unsettled. I'd never felt so alone in a crowd before.

I think what made it so difficult for my husband and me was the sense we didn't fit anywhere. We were not fans of small groups, but we tried to adapt. We attended a few, we hosted a couple, and I even led two groups through the years. We missed the mid-size offerings. We didn't fit into the seniors' group, and we didn't meet the qualifications for the young marrieds or the parents of teens either. All we wanted was to be with our church family and find community and friendships that naturally take place when meeting together in one place. We felt like outsiders in our own church family. Maybe we were.

The frustrations were mounting. As the joy I once knew continued to drain from my heart, a thick sludge of doubt and disappointment began to creep in to take its place. If this was what church was about now, I wasn't sure it was where I should be. I was certain it wasn't where I wanted to be. I wasn't sure I could support the idea of church for much longer.

I was weary from the battles and I was tired of not feeling like I was home. Tracy and I kept asking ourselves, "Why is it so hard to feel like we belong here?" We did have a small group of friends, but I questioned if we were noticed and considered a part of this church family.

In fact, there were numerous occasions when we had things happen in our lives and we were left feeling invisible. Normally, someone from the staff would pray with people before a surgery, but when my husband broke his elbow, nobody came to sit with me or called to pray with either of us. We weren't asked if we needed help with lawn care during recovery, or if finances would be okay while he was off work for almost two months. One card came.

In our years there, we had about ten times when significant life hardships, illness, deaths, or trials hit us. Those were the times when people knew what was happening and we thought they would reach out with meals, cards, visits, or prayers. It's what I knew church should be and what I understood wasn't going to happen for our family. We had one time when someone reached out during a trial to assist us, and it is a memory we treasure still. When my husband's mother died suddenly, we found ourselves making an unplanned, and unbudgeted, road trip to California at Christmas time. We were given a small gift card for gas by our current pastor.

Why Does This Hurt So Much?

It wasn't just us that seemed to be overlooked. I watched as the needs were repeatedly met for selected members, but not others. It felt like there were a few favorites while so many were left to fend for themselves. Later, when my job was eliminated, we felt invisible, with no support from what had been our church for eighteen years. Our friends were there for us, but it felt like the church leadership and members were not. Not a single staff member or elder ever contacted me to thank me for the years of service, or to check on us. We were not asked if we needed prayer, or any financial or food assistance. I did not hear, "I was sorry to hear about your job being eliminated. I'll miss working with you." Even when they released the budget information to the church, they didn't use my name but only stated that the position of Volunteer Coordinator was eliminated. Most people didn't even realize what my job title was, they only knew they interacted with me often. This was one of the most hurtful times there, but God was quick to remind us that we'd been praying for release from that job.

The disappointments were stacking up on a faith base that was no longer solid. Each one brought a heavy weight that made it increasingly difficult to stand upright. The staff meetings spent on menial topics. Church services I dreaded. Differing values on personal development. Lies from leaders. Key staff transitioned out, the ones I shared similar values with. Members left. An avoidance to innovation. My voice and vision being silenced. The pros and cons list of staying in that job or leaving was getting quite lopsided on the tally marks.

I knew it was inevitable, that someday it would become unbearable, and no hope would remain. I sensed I was transitioning into disillusionment, but I refused to give up hope for this church. I pressed on, slowly lowering my expectations, and striving to keep my head in the sand. This worked for a while. Eventually the disappointments grew too heavy and as disillusionment reared its ugly head, it brought along its good friend, destruction.

While I thought I had successfully buried the fallout from my childhood church split, I couldn't deny the impact of what happened in March 2011. I faced my second church split, this time from the viewpoint of a staffer. The cause was different, but it was just as ugly, hurtful, and divisive. Like the split in my childhood church, there was a similar Sunday when things got heated. Some memories are etched in my mind more than a decade later, while I can't recall other details.

I woke with a pit in my stomach the Sunday I knew they were announcing that my boss, Kurt, had resigned. His decision to walk away was going to catch a lot of people off guard. It was effective immediately. He was already gone. There would be no saying goodbye for the church members, no cookie social to honor his years of work and send him and his wife, Julie, off to their next adventure.

When I started working for him, he was the minister of spiritual maturity. Several years before this, our lead pastor at that time had announced plans to retire. The plan was to transition to Kurt becoming the lead pastor. Instead, a leadership team of three was formed, with Kurt being the primary. Our long-term lead pastor remained as part of the team instead of retiring, and a third pastor joined the team. It was complicated, but suffice it to say, many people viewed Kurt as a lead pastor at the time of this resignation. This news was going to be a surprise to most. Tracy and I usually sat on the main floor, about halfway back from the stage. That Sunday we sat in the balcony, behind the soundboard, attempting to go unnoticed as we waited.

As Kurt's assistant, I knew people would be looking for my reaction. I was still grieving. I didn't have anything left of myself to offer others who would soon be hearing the news. With tears streaming silently down my face the entire time, we made it through the worship music, communion, prayers, and a sermon before things took a turn. At the conclusion of the sermon, the lead elder made a quiet and unemotional announcement about the resignation. He gave the basic information that Kurt had resigned effective immediately. I'm told this update was received smoothly during the first service.

As this started to unfold at the second service, a lone woman stood up near the back of the auditorium's main floor. It was eerily silent, and the tension felt like a thick fog. A soft, yet determined voice carried across the audience, as she made eye contact with those on stage. In a pleading tone she spoke three words, "Speak the truth."

There were accusations calling people out for putting a spin on the truth or using manipulative tactics. People cried out asking, "Where is Kurt to explain?"

A man to my left stood up, and with a finger thrust in anger and frustration toward one of the leadership team pastors, exclaimed, "You drove him out!" He was in the front row of the balcony where everybody could see and hear him clearly.

From there, we had a couple of other leaders on stage who tried to settle things down. At one point, my friend Dana from the worship team went to sit beside the one who had been yelled at. Much of the anger was directed at him and you could see him physically folding inward as the shouts came. The truth was, he did carry a lot of the blame for the actions that led up to Kurt's decision. He didn't deserve the words of animosity shouted at him that day.

WHY DOES THIS HURT SO MUCH?

We were a people divided. Countless families walked out. Many never returned to that building. Some knew what the truth was. Others thought they knew, which was dangerous. Most people felt hurt, while a few were too far removed from the details to notice. Some have yet to attend church again anywhere. There were truths spoken and there were lies. Many blindly believed the lies without searching for truth.

There were no public accusations of wrong behavior. This divisive Sunday was a result of Kurt's sudden decision to leave the congregation immediately. Technically, there shouldn't have been an uproar. It certainly wasn't expected to go sideways. I was closer to the details than many, but it can be summarized by saying he reached a breaking point. Kurt was done with the games some people were playing. It wasn't a temper-tantrum, it was a choice he made based on facts and rocky transitioning. From my perspective, it was reached because of some poor leadership and the manipulative actions of some. The final straw was when one of the leaders questioned Kurt's integrity, stating he had not informed leadership about a scheduled ministry event. Weary of fighting battles that weren't based in truth, he decided to leave. I had clear evidence to refute the last lie spoken about him, an email with a response from the person who said he had not been notified. I took the truth to leadership and asked for counsel to process this. The next day in a staff meeting, the person who made the accusation, played it down as something some of us "may have misunderstood." There it was, a spin, yet again to protect his image. It will forever haunt me to know that honesty and integrity was not always the foundation of some in leadership there.

The turbulence leading up to this was based on the same thing as in any split: human nature. Within the leadership, there were lies, pride, controlling behavior, and poor communication. Thankfully, there was truth spoken years later and apologies from some involved, but not all. This did not make future pastor transitions easy. After the split, leadership transitioned to the elders, and then to two sequential new lead pastors before the current pastor stayed on. It was a rocky ride those last years I was on staff. I still see wounded people around me as many of us continue to heal. The ministry impact was huge, and the damage is still evident. Many of the ministries we had in place are no longer functioning and the size of the congregation is greatly diminished.

From the time I started working there, our leadership had changed significantly. Most of the leaders I related to, the people I shared ministry styles and worldviews with, had already left or were no longer serving. I drew on my faith and my training. I felt empowered by what I had learned through the early years of leadership development and pastoral mentoring. While hesitant, I believed I was to be the last voice speaking up for some of the things we had once stood united for as a staff. The remaining staff included many who had once prioritized the very things I tried to bring up. We were still responsible for a congregation. We were becoming outdated and would soon be ineffective. The time to do something was now.

I tried. My voice would not be heard. There would be no changes coming. In my opinion, we had become a church that looked inward, not outward. We had become a church of complacency. We were choosing the easy instead of pursuing the challenges. There are many examples in the leadership circuit where they compare a local church congregation to the football team in a huddle. Nobody attends a football game to watch people huddle. They are there to watch the game. I thought we had huddled up, only looking inward instead of playing the game. This was the heaviest weight of them all and played a big role in why I eventually gave up on church. I questioned if God was worth enduring this much disappointment for.

Division. Invisibility. Disappointment. In the Bible, Samson is said to have been able to lift mountains. Each of these burdens placed such a significant weight on my heart, I don't think even he could have lifted them. I felt the familiar rumble as the foundation began to crack beneath me again. As it crept toward the surface, I kept moving forward, believing God had called me to continue being His voice. I fought Him on that. I told Him He was wrong. I was not relevant enough to present His desires to this leadership. I was tired. I was wounded. I was done. He placed song lyrics from Chris Tomlin in front of me instead. "I Will Follow" reminded me to trust God and be willing to stay or go, depending on His call to me. It was a glorious reminder to keep following God, even in my disappointment.

I stayed. I grew empty, my trust wavered, my faith was drying out, but I stayed. More people left. Several people asked me why I didn't leave. My friend Dana continued to inquire, "What's it going to take for you to leave?" She loved me and was checking on my emotional, spiritual, and physical well-being by asking me when I was going to say enough is enough and leave my job. She knew it was destroying me. We still laugh about that one. We all need that kind of friend.

In my fifteen years employed there, I worked with more than fifty different paid staff. That is a lot of transition for a church now numbering less than 300. This was no longer the church I discovered in 2000. I knew if I left, my husband and I would likely leave church altogether due to the emotional trauma and damage from my time spent on staff. I had never had any kind of anxiety issues before, but during those last eight years I was having panic attacks frequently from the stress and felt I couldn't breathe. Eventually I didn't recognize myself. I had become someone I didn't know; a mere shell of the woman God created me to be. Disappointment is exhausting. Disillusionment is crippling.

Chapter 11

WOULD I DO THIS AGAIN?

I'VE REPEATEDLY HAD PEOPLE ASK ME two different questions. Some will ask, "Knowing what you know now, would you have taken the job?" Others ask me, "Would you choose to work a church job again?" The answer to both is the same.

No.

Not likely.

Maybe.

ABSOLUTELY NOT!

Perhaps.

Probably.

I could choose to answer that question with my gut instinct, based solely on my personal experiences, without prayerfully consulting God to see what His plans are. If I did that, the quick, knee-jerk answer would be a resounding, "NO!" NO, as in, there isn't a book big enough to contain the font size I want to use here. A billboard doesn't exist that is large enough or a font bold enough to capture the emphasis I would put on those two letters. There isn't enough breath in all of earth's residents combined to hold out the note of "N-O-O-O-O-O-" long enough to feel as if it conveys the full emotion behind that little word.

Now that the emotional response has been noted, let me share the logical side of my brain's response to that question. I had several great years and one decent year before things changed. Many years brought distance to my relationship with God and doubt in people. On top of that, I added bouts of anxiety with a side of grief. I would even toss in a touch of PTSD, trauma, and there was some spiritual abuse. I don't know many people who would have chosen to stay through those last years. I'm not sure I would choose to do it again if I knew then what I know now. It was a tough journey with a lot of heartache and scars.

Yet, my life has been positively impacted significantly in ways I'm certain would not have happened had I not naïvely answered, "Yes" when first asked, "Would you like to work here?"

Let me get back to you with an answer later.

Section Three

SPIRITUALLY UNDISCIPLINED

Who I Thought I Was

God, you waited for me to discover that I didn't have to check all the boxes on some mythical faith checklist. You waited for me to grow, so I could approach you through freedom, and not restrictions. You waited for me to understand I was exempt from the expectations of others, and what they thought my faith should look like. You waited to rescue me from religion so You could restore me to relationship once I learned that faith is about You.

Thank you for waiting.

Chapter 12
THE SILENT AMEN

THREE WORDS. THREE SEEMINGLY INNOCENT WORDS when used individually. When they are strung together in a particular order, they have the power to strike a fear in me that takes my breath away. I know I'm not alone. A complete, paralyzing terror comes over me when I hear the words, "Will you pray?" as the person looks at me expectantly. They are anticipating a "yes" response. It's not coming.

The context doesn't change things at all. This can take place in a staff meeting, Bible study class, or a small group. It won't have a different outcome if I'm with a few friends at lunch or meeting quietly with one friend needing prayer. I grew up in a church where only the men prayed publicly. This was due to a doctrinal belief that women should not pray in the presence of men. I left before I was old enough to be in a gathering of women and experience them praying. This history is likely what started my inability to pray aloud in front of others. I simply had not done it.

I have had many conversations with people who are as terrified of praying aloud with others as I am. They did not have the same church history as me, so I guess I can't use that easy explanation as my defense. I think we sometimes find ourselves intimidated when we listen to others pray. It's easy to elevate people who can pray comfortably in public to an imaginary pedestal we can't reach. We sometimes hold them up as examples and may even label them a "good" Christian. The concept of a good Christian is an ideal some may strive toward, but nobody can live up to that. It's not a biblical concept.

I hate to admit this, but as hard as I try, I rarely stay focused when others are praying. I listen, then find I'm busy making a mental note of an errand I need to run. I refocus, I listen, I make plans for lunch. I promise God I'll listen better. I listen again momentarily, then I get restless. The cycle continues. I'm not proud of that, but I know a lot of us do this. I usually toss in a bit of self-condemnation for not being a better Christian as I compare myself to the one praying.

On the other hand, there are a few people I know whose prayers draw me in. I feel like I could listen for hours. Well, maybe not for HOURS, but I can certainly lose track of time while they pray. It's as if they are talking with someone they love dearly, and I've been invited to an intimate and beautiful conversation. It's never about what they say or how they say it. It's never about the topic of the prayer. It's not that they are better at praying than others or are any closer to God. I believe it is all about their relationship with Him, and the resulting style of how they approach our Father. It's one that happens to resonate with me. It is what my heart longs for and I admire it when I see it. Somehow their words seem a little more special, richer, and more connected with God. I am grateful to experience God through their eyes, and their prayers.

We also see people who are so comfortable with prayer, they instantly take time to pray with each opportunity, regardless of how many people might be present. It is as natural to them to turn to prayer in the moment as it is for the rest of us to breathe. I hope we all get to experience this kind of prayer life for ourselves. It is a wonderful thing to strive for, but it cannot be forced. For those of us whose prayers don't come naturally, that's okay. We are normal. We are not lesser Christians. God doesn't love us less.

Maybe prayer has become a task or chore on our list. Maybe it haunts us as we listen to the eloquent prayers of others. Prayer can be intimidating, but that's because we have lost sight of what it really is. Our human nature is to compare, but God never compares His kids to each other. He made each of us to be unique and He delights in that. Deep down, we know this, but it is so easy to ignore the truth and believe the lies comparison brings. Most of us have been listening to them for too many years. The power of comparison is stronger than we realize, but God has the ability to remove that stumbling block. Maybe we should consider praying about that.

When I took the job at my church, I was newly returned to my faith and had not yet developed any spiritual disciplines. Prayer had never been a regular part of my life and I was now spending my work hours surrounded by people who I believed fit the profile for model Christians. I knew I could never pray aloud in front of them, and I had no desire to attempt it. Sometimes we would break off into groups of two to three for prayer after staff meetings. Even worse than that was when all the women would stay together for prayer time. It was the same each time. We'd gather together, pull our chairs in close to each other, and decide who would start the prayers and who would close. I'd avert my eyes and judge myself as inferior while I quietly spoke, "Remember, I'm not going to be praying." I don't believe I was ever judged for it, and eventually I no longer had to face the humiliation of saying it. They knew I would always opt out of praying, and I knew I would always feel like I was less than the others in God's eyes.

Occasionally, I would be walking stronger in my faith and be ready to pray with one other person. Invariably, that would be the same day when a co-worker would toss out, "Maybe this will be the day Lois will pray," and that's all it took to shut things down. I was NOT going to do it now with all that extra pressure on me. She had no way of knowing that would hurt me and probably thought she was encouraging me, but it had the opposite effect.

The staff knew I wasn't comfortable praying aloud. While a few gently encouraged me and challenged me to work on growing in this area, I could rest in knowing it wouldn't be forced. This also let me accept that I would not be called on in a group setting to pray. Oh, what glorious peace!

Then we transitioned leadership. Jon, the new lead pastor, would call on people to pray at staff meetings, and he did not ask for volunteers. I was certain I was going to have to quit my job. It was humiliating, but I had to go tell Jon I was not willing to pray aloud in front of others. As I sat across the desk from him, I looked him in the eye and asked, "Will it be a problem for me to remain on staff if I won't pray aloud?" He didn't hesitate with his response. His words were assuring, "That won't be an issue. I appreciate you coming to me and sharing that."

He went on to encourage me to consider working toward praying, but didn't judge me for it. He knew it would be good for my relationship with God. Whew!

Then we transitioned leadership again. I held my breath as I approached the same office for the identical conversation, this time with Chris, where I begged not to be called upon for prayer at the staff meetings. He told me it wasn't a problem and I could stay on staff. Whew!

I wanted desperately to be a person who was comfortable praying with others, but by now I felt as if it had become part of my identity. I had added a new label to define me; I'm the one who won't pray. I continued to compare myself, always coming up short, and eventually complacency settled in and I no longer cared to try to grow in my prayer life.

I vividly recall the first time I had someone point blank ask me to pray over them. Barb was a new friend at the time and had asked me to visit with her as she was going through a bit of something and needed to talk. Of course, I went rushing over there, no questions asked. I've often been in situations when people have shared something and asked me to pray for them. I can confidently assure them I will. They will become a part of my prayer list and I will check in on them for a while until things settle or the prayer is answered. I may even send them a card.

This time was different. After we talked for a while, I heard those three familiar words I fear so intensely, "Will you pray?" I was rehearsing my usual response of, "Of course I'll be praying for you," when I heard her continue with, "over me now." It felt like I'd forgotten how to breathe. I didn't know how I would be able to pray, but Barb was a friend, and so I prayed. You know what? I didn't die. I have no idea if it was eloquent or if I bumbled my way through incoherently, but she was important to me and so we prayed together. She thanked me, we hugged, and I went to my car and cried. I still felt inferior, but I felt my bond with God grow stronger.

I'd like to tell you this was a moment of spiritual epiphany but I'm not writing a fiction book. To this day, when people have needs and ask me to pray, I get that sick feeling in the pit of my stomach. I will pray diligently for them, but it still won't be in front of them. That only happened the one time, and I don't know when or if I will ever be able to do this joyfully and willingly. I also know God hears our prayers regardless of who else does. I understand how meaningful it is to hear someone pray for you and I've been blessed deeply to have a few people do that for me. This is why I continue to struggle with guilt when a friend asks me to pray. I'm afraid they are waiting for the prayer to begin. My words are not coming. I then don't believe I deserve to hear words of prayer spoken on my behalf when I need it. This is a terrible place to be. I hope, and pray, we will all grow into the kind of prayer life that can support others.

Prayer was not something that came naturally to me. Maybe it's the same way for you. I heard it done formally in church services several times each week and it was always done before meals. I knew prayer could be done alone or privately and may be unspoken or verbalized. None of these were a common practice for me. Prayer simply had not become something I did frequently on my own. We're probably all familiar with the phrase "spiritual disciplines" and know that prayer is always listed as one of those. I've even heard it referred to as the most important one. Because praying may not feel natural, it might take some time before you feel comfortable to adopt this spiritual discipline. It's okay if trying to develop a prayer life is a difficult step to take. There are numerous reasons for that, and I hope we can work together to overcome some of those because it is important.

We have several opportunities to step into a life of prayer and they aren't all public or terrifying. In fact, most of the time I spend in prayer now isn't witnessed by anybody other than God. He designed prayer to be an open invitation to hang out and chat with Him. I've learned a lot about prayer recently, and I look forward to sharing more in the last section of this book. For now, I want to plant a few seeds with you.

If you want to step into prayer and see what can happen, here are a few things I've come across that might be useful. Time can stand still when trying something new, but what if you used a timer to help? Don't be overly ambitious or set unrealistic expectations like trying to pray for an hour on the first day. Start small but start. God doesn't have a time requirement. Begin with one minute and see how things go. Gradually, you could increase this as you find yourself becoming comfortable with the act of praying.

If you struggle with remembering topics, prepare yourself before you begin praying. Write down a few things that have been on your mind recently. It's okay to open your eyes while praying and you can refer to this list if you get anxious. You can always turn to a scripture or the Lord's Prayer as a starting point. Try reading the lyrics from some favorite songs or hymns. I love music and there are so many songs that would be good for initiating a time of prayer. We all have favorites that hit us just so, right where the Holy Spirit is working. Embrace it and go talk to the Father about how it made you feel. Try keeping a prayer journal and use that to talk through. After all, prayer is just a conversation.

I would encourage you to not put the pressure on yourself to do this daily as you are starting. Once a week will take the worry and fear off your shoulders and it will naturally expand into more. Prayer is so much more than I ever understood it to be. I want the relationship for you that I'm developing with God because of my new discovery of prayer.

I hear a lot about people who have designed their homes to provide a place marked out for prayer. This isn't necessary. God is with us everywhere and hears us at any time. But there are many reasons this could be beneficial. If your life schedule is hectic or your home is a busy place, maybe your closet or the bathroom is your quiet sanctuary for a few minutes with God. I read a sweet little book one time where the lead character had a prayer chair. It was an oversized, super soft, cozy upholstered chair, and it was her designated place. If she was in her chair, she was praying. Find what works for you. It doesn't matter what anybody else is doing.

We all struggle sometimes, wondering what to say. We know God already knows what's going on, but like an earthly parent, He wants to hear it from us. I was once attending a women's Bible study group where the leader guided us through painting an image in our minds. It was so vivid that it has stuck with me for over two decades. She had us imagine ourselves as children coming home from a long day at school. I'd like to tell you to close your eyes as I describe this, but I realize you can't read that way. Instead, I will ask you to read through these sentences slowly, stopping to absorb each one and visualize yourself in this setting. I'll do it with you.

We are young children, maybe grade school age, just getting off the school bus or at the end of our walk home after the last bell has rung. As we walk up the sidewalk to the house, we see an adult, or perhaps an older sibling, waiting for us on the porch. Maybe it's our mom or grandma sitting there with a plate of cookies and some lemonade. She's been anticipating this moment for twenty minutes, anxious to hear all about our day. As we take a cookie and plop ourselves down on the chair next to her, she asks us, "What was your favorite part of school today? What did you learn?" Most of us have an answer ready for the favorite part, but it might take a second cookie as we recall what we learned that day. Maybe it's a dad instead. As we move from the chair to his lap, he inquires, "What did you have for lunch today? Did you have fun at recess?" As we nod our heads enthusiastically, we reach for the lemonade. That's when he notices the dirt and the bruise on our knee. With a hint of concern in his voice, he asks, "How did you scrape your knee?"

It doesn't matter what any of our answers are. In fact, they can probably guess most of our answers before they even ask. Nothing brings them more joy than hearing it from us directly. They want to be included in our day. I often see God waiting for me on the front porch, eager to hear me tell Him anything and everything. He likes to hear my voice. He likes to hear your voice. Our voices are like music to His ears, and He knows them because He created them.

As long as we are praying about things He would find acceptable, that don't go against His very nature, I don't think we can pray incorrectly. We understand that His answers vary and include, "Yes," "No," and "Wait." It's okay to pray repeatedly for things. I'm not beyond begging at times. I do prefer to think of it as calling out to Him, but I'm willing to admit it's pretty much begging. I still think He's tickled to hear from me, and He doesn't object to my repetitiveness.

What about you? Where do you stand on your approach to prayer? If you have it nailed, that's great! Would you consider taking someone under your wing and mentoring them in prayer? We aren't all confident in this, whether it is done in the quiet of our bedroom or in a group setting. It's scary to some of us. I've been a Christian since I was eleven and I'm only just now figuring things out.

If you are intrigued with the idea of hanging out with God and sharing what's on your heart but are still apprehensive, find someone you trust and ask them to help you become more comfortable with the idea. Is there somebody you relate to when they pray? Reach out to them. Ask them how they feel toward God when they are praying.

If you are still feeling like this is one of those yucky discipline things and you don't like being told what you should do, I feel you. Oh boy, do I feel you! I can remember walking down the hallway to do my homework after school. Sometimes Dad would casually inquire, "Do you have any homework today?" The minute he did, it felt like it was no longer my idea, and it would frustrate me. I have never liked being told to do something. I'm a bit stubborn that way. However, know you aren't alone in thinking this way. I was there, too. I will forever be grateful that I'm learning about the far deeper connection and purpose of prayer. I'll touch again on this in the last section as I share with you the impact prayer has made in my life. Stick around, try to keep an open mind, and let's see if we can do this prayer thing together. Start practicing now.

Chapter 13
GATHERING DUST

PEOPLE HAVE BEEN TEACHING ME ABOUT GOD for several decades. It began in my childhood Sunday School classes where the ladies would teach us Bible stories using flannel boards with character cutouts. Adulthood has included its fill of sermons, classes, seminars, online resources, and small groups. Somewhere along the way, I came to understand that we are supposed to read the Bible for ourselves in addition to these formal teachings. At a minimum, we should at least want to read it.

I have it downloaded on my phone, tablet, Kindle, and computer. You may think this makes me look like a super-committed "Gold Star Christian." Be careful about comparisons, looks can be deceiving. I own numerous Bibles in a variety of versions, sizes, colors, font sizes, and formats. Some were gifts, and others I purchased myself. Usually, those purchases were made while proclaiming,

"NOW I'll start reading the Bible because I have the RIGHT one." I have huge, heavy study Bibles and lightweight, more portable ones. Some of them are basic paperbacks, while several are beautiful masterpieces and emit the rich aroma of leather. I have always been a sucker for the smell of leather. I blame my childhood days of a life spent around baseball mitts, cowboy boots, and saddles.

Sadly, when it comes time to pick one of these Bibles up to use, I find I must first dust it off. For far too many years, this occurred only once, the week before the annual church staff retreat. Because they are unused, I couldn't tell you exactly where any of them are right now. They are scattered on a variety of bookshelves in multiple rooms. I usually put one where I think I'll reach for it but never do. I can't find any of them quickly.

Was I ever inspired to read my Bible, other than to occasionally review a particular scripture from a class or sermon? I can't say that I was. Did a preacher ever create the desire in me to read the Bible? No. An elder? No. A youth pastor? No. A ministry leader? No. Was any Bible study class so exciting that I went rushing to get my Bible ready? No.

Yet today, I can now say I have read through the entire Bible. Was I forced to do it? No. Did I lose a bet? No. Was I financially rewarded for doing so? No.

So, what happened? Why now? I met a police officer. Then I met a second officer. No, I wasn't arrested and converted on the way to jail, although it wouldn't have been a first for either officer. I was part of a non-profit that served first responders, and I went on a ride-along to gain a better understanding of what the job looks like. This was where I met Tom. Later, I met his friend, Jason. Both men were Christians. Through the years of serving in that ministry, I formed friendships with several wonderful officers. Tom and Jason were two friends who challenged me regularly in my faith, encouraging me to grow and deepen my connection with God. While I was texting with them on an unrelated topic, God started to impress upon my heart the idea of reading the Bible. Both men regularly shared insights from what they had read, and I was tired of nodding in agreement to things I only had a vague recollection of from my childhood Bible stories.

The staff at the non-profit had recently spent two years reading through the books of James and Mark at our weekly staff meetings. As we read through and discussed those books, I found I was experiencing a slow-growing interest in reading the Bible. I wasn't ready to commit to it, but I was ready to entertain the idea of considering praying for God to create the desire to want to even want to read the Bible. Simultaneously, I found myself fighting the overwhelming and deep-seated need and yearning to read it. I realized I was slowly losing the stories I learned growing up. I panicked. What kind of Christian worked for a faith-based non-profit AND a church but had never read the Bible? I asked Linda, my co-worker friend, to keep me in her prayers. Specifically, I asked her to pray that God would create a desire in me to want to read the Bible.

Jason, one of my Christian police friends, stopped by my office one day. He's the same one I mentioned before who asked me about our church services being biblical. We were having a great conversation about several of the more controversial topics currently impacting the church, when I mentioned I was looking for "my truth" on some of these. I meant I wanted to be confident about where I stood. I knew I needed to know it was my own belief, based on my biblical understanding. I had a fear of mirroring what I'd been taught by my parents and church leaders growing up. It was important to me to also be certain my belief wasn't being undermined by the current church and society pressure to accept any and all lifestyles, without biblical accountability. I was looking for where **I** stood in my beliefs. It's a semantics thing. But his words were wise, as usual. He simply pointed out I needed to find "THE" truth and not "my" truth. I could respect that, and it really was what I was trying to say.

Then he continued, "There's only one way to know God, and that's to spend time in His word." Then a gentle question to me, "How are you doing with your time in the Word?"

I did not want to answer. This was going to be humiliating. I dropped my head in shame, refused to make eye contact, and slowly answered truthfully. "Jason, I don't remember the last time I opened my Bible."

I went home and spent three days looking for a Bible.

I am convinced God puts the right people in our life at the right time, and there is always a greater purpose woven in. It has happened to me far too many times to think of ever disputing this concept. At this point in my life, there were only two or three people I couldn't snowball with an answer that would have been completely truthful, completely deceptive, and what they wanted to hear; all while maintaining a good image and making me feel good.

Jason was one of those I could not bluff. Nor would I want to. For most of the rest of you, my answer would have been something like, "I recently finished reading James and Mark and I even have the Bible downloaded on my phone." All true, but relatively meaningless. All equally untrue as it relates to the question. Those first responder ministry staff meetings were opened with a Bible reading each week and it took us almost two years to read through two books. Just because I have the Bible app on my phone doesn't mean I use it. I believe he would have seen right through me, even if I had tried to bluff him.

When my grandfather died, we found numerous Bibles in his home, but there was one that stood out, one that was obviously his everyday Bible. The cover was worn, and the pages were frayed, written on, and highlighted. This was the one that showed how vital God's word was to his daily life. The evidence of that was reflected in the way he lived his life. I now have that Bible. At the time, it moved me to purchase a new Bible with the goal of it becoming like his. My hope was that one day when I'm gone, somebody would find it and know how I must have lived my life. This is the same Bible it took me three days to find. I sometimes worry its pristine condition will indeed reflect how I lived my life.

I was mistaken in my view of the Bible. I believed the Old Testament was only a history book and the New Testament was a guide to living a good Christian life, with a lot of history. I loathe history and prefer to live in the moment, looking forward, rather than looking back. It didn't make any difference if that history was recorded in the Bible. I also felt like I knew what I should be doing to live out the Christian walk. All of this contributed to my lack of desire to read the Bible. When you add in the lifelong pulpit commands to read the Bible, to have a quiet time, and to keep a journal, I'm ready to put up the walls of rebellion. I don't like being told what to do. I prefer to think of doing things of my own accord. Remember, I can be too independent for my own good.

Let me tell you, I couldn't have been more wrong about what the Bible is and the value of spending time reading it. It was a humbling experience to read it and realize there were some fundamental basics I could not remember, relate to, or understand. I discovered early in the reading process that I needed to humble myself, have friends praying for me through this time, and approach it as a child or a new believer. After all, this was a new endeavor for me. I would soon discover I had a lot to learn.

I had a safe, non-judgmental friend in Jason. He was excited for me and happy to allow me to ask anything. Because I grew up with Bible knowledge and was so much older than Jason, I considered most of my questions to be dumb. It was a bit humiliating to ask such simple questions of someone so much younger than me, but God does give us wise friends of all ages. I think we should all look for those we can trust around us and not be too proud to ask for help. The lesson in humility was priceless. The distance between me and God started closing, and it was worth it all.

What made a lifelong anti-Bible reader choose to read through the entire Bible? The answer still surprises me. It started with social media. I was part of a Facebook group of women in leadership. Shortly after joining it, they kicked off a 90-Day Read Through the Bible Challenge for summer. My first thought was, "It's only ninety days. Maybe I could do this. It's not like it will take all year to read through it like all those other reading plans out there."

At the same time, there was a creativity-based, 60-Day challenge that would be the happy reward while enduring the reading. Yes, enduring. I expected this to be torture. I didn't really want to do it, but I knew I should. Both challenges started simultaneously. Before I began, I gave myself permission to read for only a week or so and quit. At least it would be a start, and perhaps a seed planted for the future. I fully expected to last less than two weeks and to miss half the days during that time. I was setting myself up with permission to bail and hide behind the "at least you tried" badge.

I had been praying for a heart's desire to be created in me for reading the Bible. I had a few others praying for this as well. God had answered those prayers; I had a plan. During my commute, I would listen to the Bible online. I could also do that while cleaning the house or folding laundry. If I could do two things at once, I might be able to do it for a week or so. I was stunned when I realized this wasn't enough for me. I wanted to see the words, feel the pages being turned. I wanted to be able to review a verse if I needed to. While I did listen to some of the readings, I chose to read over 90% of it instead.

I found myself arriving at meetings, lunches, and appointments early with the deliberate intention of being able to sit and read while I waited! I went to bed early so I could read longer each night. We're talking about thirty to fifty minutes of reading each day. I found myself anxiously anticipating it, almost aching for the time when I would get to read. I loved the challenge of checking off each chapter on the list and enjoyed watching my reading streak get longer. If I am issued a challenge, or told I can't do something, stand back, and watch me. I will prove myself.

While this is a lot to take on, I would strongly encourage you to find something that you can stick with. For some of you it is the traditional reading plan, but for others you need something outside the box. Go find what works for you and start. Start. Now. Like the other spiritual disciplines, there is no right or wrong way to read, but I now understand it is a necessity for every believer to read the Bible.

As I started reading, I began doubting my own faith and trust in God, again. As I read about the wrath of God, the deaths, the suffering, and the punishment that was so prevalent then, I found myself doubting and questioning. This was the first question I texted to Jason. "How can that God be the same God we're supposed to love?" For the first time, I could completely relate to people who doubt His love, goodness, and approachability.

As I continued reading, I came to understand the concept of fearing God. I could not relate to this before. Why would I fear a God who loves me unconditionally? I finally grasped that we should fear God for what He is capable of. It is more of a respect and awareness that also leads to a deeper love and gratitude. For believers, the joy comes when we realize we no longer need to fear God's wrath, because of His promise and gift of salvation through the death of Jesus Christ. However, the day will come when many do need to fear Him, if they have not chosen a life of obedience.

During this time of reading, Tom, my other police officer friend, told me, "I want to buy you a Bible." He asked me to pick out a few I was interested in and let him know. The only way I could convey the firestorm this created in me would be to write page after page of the conversations I had in my mind, along with the dozens of texts and emails back and forth between us so you could see the struggle. I didn't receive this gift easily and I must admit my pride stood in the way.

Gathering Dust

I already had several Bibles I wasn't using, but of course, I didn't want to admit that to him and blow my image of being a proper Christian. Mostly, I didn't want him to spend his money on me, as I wasn't used to receiving gifts. Also, I could be pretty picky about things like that. I had just barely reached the age when font size began to matter to my aging eyes. The thickness of the pages, so the words didn't bleed through, was also becoming more important. However, I didn't want to admit that to him either. I would always choose leather, but there was no way I was going to tell someone about my expensive preferences when he was the one making the purchase. Add to this the fact that he was technically young enough to be my kid, and I should have been the more spiritually mature one. It was a perfect storm.

I didn't feel worthy to receive such a gift. I didn't know how to accept it. While I've always longed to be noticed and hoped to be on the receiving end of kind acts, I had become used to this not happening. Looking back, I think maybe I wanted people to think of me, even wanted them to be kind and generous, but I didn't want them to follow through and make me the focus. It was quite a comical event, which, once again brought me to the great and wonderful place of humility. But it was a painful journey. I tried to ignore him. Even as I write this, I must laugh. I have met a lot of people over the course of my lifetime and he is one of the top few who would not accept being ignored when it comes to sharing about God.

3,776 words. This is how long the final, "I give up, you can give me a Bible; here are the ones I like, but you choose" email was. That's longer than this chapter, and it was only the final email, when I surrendered and accepted his beautiful gift.

Chapter 14
PULL UP A CHAIR

SHH. DO YOU HEAR THAT? It's the sound of quiet. The frightening and eerie, yet obsessively sought-after soundtrack for the spiritual discipline referred to as a quiet time with God. Sometimes I can't hear it above the roar within my own heart and mind. When I can still myself enough to hear it, it startles me. It is unfamiliar and uncomfortable. Quiet means I'm alone with my thoughts, giving the Holy Spirit an open door to really get involved. Often when I am faced with this stillness, I want to whisper, "Make the silence stop." Sometimes I don't welcome it, often I won't embrace it.

While there are many spiritual disciplines, this is the one that has always posed the biggest challenge for me. Not only does it require me to be still and quiet, but it also draws from several other actions that I have yet to perfect, or even to desire to incorporate. I'm not one to sit and watch a movie without working on a secondary task. Quiet stresses me. When a puppy or small child is quiet, it is almost a guarantee that something's not going well. I thought the same thing about approaching a quiet time. I flat out did not want to do it and I knew it wouldn't go well.

When I was first learning about this new activity, it seemed the phrase "quiet time" had an implied third word in its title. I always heard about how a Christian is supposed to have a *daily* quiet time with God. Also, it carried with it an assumed expectation that this would be done in the mornings, often in the early mornings. Three strikes against me already! I'm not good with schedules, so here I was, facing a daily activity at my worst time of day. It was going to require an earlier start than the normal morning routine. Using this definition, I expected failure before I tried.

There were plenty of sources telling me what I needed to include for a quiet time to be considered successful. I should be praying, reading my Bible, journaling, sitting quietly, and memorizing Bible verses. I would need to have study guides, Bible handbooks, multiple Bible versions, cross-referencing books, notepads, pens, and highlighters on hand. Then there would be more prayer, more stillness, and more quiet before I could stop. I wasn't going to get a "well done" from God on this one. Somewhere along my life's journey I developed a pattern of not doing something at all if I couldn't do it perfectly. I know, I know. That's not a great pattern. But it was the way I did, or didn't do things, so I tended to skip out on quiet time completely, since I knew I wouldn't do it correctly.

I was convinced I was the only church employee in all of history to fail the quiet-time test. Almost every day, someone would refer to something they had read, memorized, journaled, or learned during their quiet time that morning. I was never able to add to those conversations, but I did perfect the deep furrowed-brow head-nod that indicated I understood quiet time and had a similar depth of experience that morning. I had mastered the ability to compare my faith to others based solely upon their outward displays. This was one area I used regularly to tell myself I was a terrible Christian, especially for a church employee, small group leader, and ministry leader. Like my inability, or unwillingness, to pray aloud, this was a secret I worked desperately to contain.

If you have mastered the personal connection with God and you enjoy quiet time, I celebrate that with you. I would ask you to consider becoming a mentor to someone. Many of us are intimidated by the thought of something seemingly so divine. There are people around you who would love to hear about what helped you grow in your dedication to this beautiful act of worship and connection with God.

If you've ever struggled with not feeling deeply connected to God and sought out a friend or pastor to have a conversation with on this topic, you probably had a similar experience to mine. It would be pointed out to me that to truly know God, I needed to be spending time with Him. I would always agree, but rarely make any attempt to modify my routine. I have heard it said that most people don't really need to learn, so much as they need to be reminded.

If we want to know God, to know what His temperament is like, what pleases Him, and what makes Him smile, we need to read His words, write them on our hearts, and value them. Yes, we need to read the Bible. I know, I didn't want to either, remember? Even after I read through all sixty-six books, it seemed that nothing stuck around in my memory. But the words were being written on my heart. I can now draw on things I know are in there, even if I can't remember where they are. That's what all those reference tools are for!

One of the hardest things for me to figure out was knowing where to start reading. I had no interest in reading the Old Testament, with the possible exception of Proverbs, which I always found intriguing. I am not a fan of history, and that's all I thought the Old Testament was good for. I was wrong about that, by the way. I felt like I had a good representation from the New Testament from so many years of sermons. I used these excuses for months, even after I knew I wanted to get into the word of God.

Finally, a friend recommended 1st John, as it is such an encouraging book. Next, he suggested I read Mark because, "It never hurts to spend time hearing about Jesus." That was helpful for me, it was as if He became real and relevant again.

I was part of a small group that was studying Hebrews, which left me feeling completely discouraged. I felt light years behind in my Bible knowledge as I listened to the group discussion. It was interesting, but I always came away feeling small. With that weighing on me, I asked my preacher friend, who led the group, for another recommendation. This time he guided me to spend time in the seventh and eighth chapters of Romans. The funny thing is my pastor had also been encouraging me to read the Book of Romans. Those are some good starts for anybody. I have always found James, Galatians, and Philippians to be very encouraging and relatable. Those are where I find myself when I need to start reading again after a long hiatus.

I think reading the Bible in chronological order would be interesting, and would tie things together, making it easier to track. Any of these will provide a good jump start and you'll find your way from there. It surprised me when I eventually found the Bible interesting, and it no longer became a chore to read. If your Bible version becomes a bit unclear when you read larger sections, pick up a simpler one for general reading purposes. If it isn't easy to comprehend, you'll stop doing it. Get one that is easy to understand and then use the other versions to cross-reference and study.

As we become more familiar with the content, verses will begin to hop off the pages and grab our hearts and minds. This is a great path to the next step, memorization. What a treasure it is to know we can find a scripture of comfort from within our own mind when tough times strike. If we are feeling defeated, we can call up a verse about God's strength or comfort, even if we can't get to a Bible to look it up. I can certainly appreciate the value of this even if I never had the desire to set out and deliberately do this. I also found it was happening unintentionally, the more that I read.

Prayer is another component you'll find in a quiet time, but perhaps with a twist from what we normally think of as prayer time. Prayer is remarkably simple and yet so complex. The simple aspect is that it can be summed up as time talking with God. That's all there is to it. It is not a difficult or complicated thing to do, and we don't have to know what we're doing to pray. But so much can be added to this simple act. The power of time spent in prayer is indescribable, therefore, complex. We know He hears our prayers, no matter what we say or how long or short they are. But do we hear Him? Yep, you guessed it. That's where the quiet comes in. We need to spend some time stilling our minds and waiting on Him so we can hear His guidance or answers.

Voices are unique. No matter what we think about spiritual disciplines, or church attendance, we should want to be so connected to God, our Father, that we clearly recognize His voice when He speaks.

I imagine a little girl lost in an enormous store, too short to see over the shelves and racks to know her parent is only three feet away and watching her every move. She eventually cries out in fear, searching for her parent's reassuring voice. She can recognize the voice and once she hears it, knows there is no reason to be afraid.

Each of us has a unique voice, and God recognizes our individual sounds. That doesn't change based on our actions. While we will always remain precious and known to Him, I sure enjoy the idea that if I'm praying to Him regularly, He will know me from the times I've chosen to spend together. I want Him to know my voice, because He has heard from me often and I want to know His voice so well that I recognize it immediately.

Journaling is another common practice to include in quiet times. There are countless study guides available that would help with creating a quiet time. You can find some that walk through specific books of the Bible with reflections and questions for you to answer. Others may be based on a topic.

I was once part of the Women's Ministry Leadership Team, where we tried to help women, hoping to encourage friendships and inspire spiritual growth. We offered a series of Girl's Night Out events that would alternate between being social or instructional; often a blend of the two. One I coordinated was about having a quiet time. As one part of that night, I did a skit about how to have a quiet time. I based it on my attempts to establish this in my own life, but I knew when I heard the reaction from the audience that I was not alone in my struggles. Neither are you.

I began by walking down the center aisle from the back of the room, carrying a large tote bag and humming. There was a desk at the front of the room, where I stopped and began unpacking as I sat down. I was narrating each action as if it was my brain talking through things, giving the reason for each item I methodically pulled out of the bag.

"First, I have my Bible for reading, along with a marker for underlining, and a complete set of assorted highlighters. That way I can make the verses that are important stand out."

As I reached for the next three items, I set them down on top of each other, forming a tall stack of heavy books. "For the major research, I brought along my giant three-inch-thick Study Bible, a concordance, and a Bible handbook."

Rounding out the "necessary components of a quiet time" were a blank notebook with three colors of pens and a map of the Bible lands, "so I won't get lost." The last item was a candle, because don't all great Christians use candles to create the mood to be quiet with Jesus? It sure seemed that way if you believed all the book covers in the Spiritual Growth section at the bookstores. In any case, it felt more reverent and more conducive to creating an atmosphere for quiet. Once settled, I started with trying to turn my mind off.

"OK Brain, it's time to settle down. I'm here to spend some quiet time with God."

My brain adamantly declared, "Fat chance! I have things to do. I don't have time to be still."

"I want to grow closer to God, and apparently this is how you do it. So, please? Can you just give me fifteen minutes of quiet?"

"No."

"Please?"

"No."

"Well, God is bigger than you, so we'll just see about that."

I then proceeded to settle in. I announced what book to read, then I made a big production about getting the highlighter ready and the pen and notebook. At that point, I was explaining that I should probably open my quiet time with prayer. Yes, I had it written out. I was terrified of praying aloud, even if it was in a skit so I thought it would help.

I apprehensively began to pray, "Dear God, I'm new to this, but I want to try to know you better. I want to thank you for your love…"

I switched gears and voices so they could hear my brain speaking up, interrupting my prayer. My brain wasn't going to give in easily and started shouting at me, "Hey! Hey! Don't forget we need to go to the grocery store tomorrow and get bread."

I determinedly tried again. "I'm sorry God, but I'm back now and would like to try again."

The brain interrupted again with a drawn out, "Hellooooo! Are you listening to me? When we go to the store, we also need to get more dog food. I know, let's take the dog with us for a ride."

It went on like this for several minutes, but the main idea behind my skit is that we all have trouble quieting our minds and clearing out the clutter of everyday life. That's okay. We have God's permission to extend ourselves some grace and patience. We are trying to find new habits, and that takes time. Let's lighten the expectation of perfection from ourselves and seek out improvement instead. Any day we have any portion of quiet time, it is good.

Next time you try to designate some time to sit and read the Bible, add a few minutes of prayer and two minutes of silence. Voilà! Quiet time. The next time, maybe read through the lyrics of your favorite worship song, then sit quietly for two minutes to see what happens before following that up with a bit of Bible reading. It's not going to hurt, I promise.

There are many components that can go into a quiet time, and they are all good things. We should consider each one as we grow in our faith. Never forget, they aren't a checklist of requirements. It might be that some work for you regularly, and others may be something new you have to slowly develop and learn. That's okay.

Chapter 15
UNWRITTEN WORDS

DO YOU REMEMBER WHEN you were a kid and first discovered magnets? I remember being fascinated that the pull was so strong; it was pointless to fight against it. I'm reminded of that unstoppable force when I walk by a quaint little gift shop, art supply store, or the rare and elusive stationers. I am immediately drawn into the building as if a magnet is pulling me. I seem to have no voice in the matter; it is going to happen, and resistance is pointless. Once I cross the threshold, it doesn't take long for me to hear that imagined, unique cry emanating from the journal section. Oh, the variety that awaits discovery! The colors and styles of journal covers seems endless. Bright solid colors. License plates and road signs. Positive affirmations. Tropical palm trees and floral bouquets. Dream and goal motivational quotes. Beaches, oceans, and islands. Some were cute and whimsical, while others were classic and sleek. Tie-to-close. Spiral-bound. Unlined. Lined. White pages. Ivory pages. Leather—I can't forget the leather ones! Can you recall the glorious warm and raw natural scent of rawhide or lambskin?

Journals are one of only a few tangible items that seem to be able to break through my stronghold of controlled, responsible spending. I don't attempt to put up a fight anymore and I easily justify their purchase because it's something that I can use to draw closer to God. Right? I always tell myself, "I'll start journaling if I buy that one. It will be different this time." If that sounds familiar, it's because it's the same approach I took about the perfect Bible.

The purchase that doesn't fit into any of my budget categories is made, my rare treat to myself. The precious journal is tucked safely into a bag and on the way home with me to face a new beginning. I glance over at it several times as I drive home. If it is purchased while on vacation, it will be packed into the carry-on bag because I couldn't possibly risk any damage to it by stowing it away in the suitcase, trusting others with this treasure. It is my newest, most-prized possession, and I somehow believe it has the magical powers to change my life.

At home, in a grand entrance fit for trumpet announcement, it is carried ever so delicately to a place of honor where I can glance at it admiringly and let the hope it brings course through me. From time to time those first few weeks, I will pick it up and turn it over repeatedly in my hands, smiling. Those beautiful blank pages make my heart skip a beat. As I run my hand over the cover, I can almost feel a shiver going down my spine. Will this be the journal of my dreams, goals, and aspirations, or maybe a place to name and count my blessings? Perhaps this will become a prayer journal or maybe the Idea Book I dream of starting. I often go so far as to entertain the idea of it being for my sermon notes or Bible study, neither of which I am actively doing. All that potential waits for me, for my written words to be forever documented. Forever. Documented. Yep, forever. Hmmm.

This is when the polished shine of expectation begins to tarnish. What if someone finds my journals after I die? Worse yet. What if they find them while I am still alive? Is it safe to put my thoughts on paper and risk the invasion of another's set of eyes? At this point, I take it down from the honored place it's been, only to toss it casually into the cute beach-themed box with the other journals of disappointment. It is time for it to take its rightful place with countless others that also once gave me the illusion I would be a better Christian if I purchased a journal.

You are likely ahead of me on this learning curve, and I hope you are. Apparently, the concept of journaling is less about purchasing them and more about writing in them. If you are in the same stage of journaling adventures as me, I hope my life lesson will save you a lot of money, disappointment, and storage issues.

We all understand the noun definition, but did you know it's also a verb? Merriam-Webster states, "To enter or record daily thoughts, experiences, etc., in a journal" and to be honest, this verb definition makes my heart happy. This tells us there really isn't an incorrect way to journal. I want to unpack that definition a bit more. If you think about it, a journal can be viewed as a tangible version of our prayers. God wants to hear from us. He wants us to tell Him our thoughts and talk about our experiences, among other things. Anything that is on our hearts or minds is important to Him and He would love to hear about it from us directly. If you approach journaling in the same manner as prayer, that might take some of the apprehension away.

I have sat through classes and heard many in leadership tell us we need to be journaling. Once again, I allow myself to feel lesser than others because I'm not ready to adopt this practice. They even refer to it as a spiritual discipline. Yikes! Everything about the phrase "spiritual discipline" rubs me the wrong way. It makes me feel as if it is necessary to do this, and I must be perfect at it. This also carries with it the weight of comparison to others. If I am not journaling daily, and doing it perfectly, then I am clearly not a good Christian. Those words have never been stated directly, but it is how I interpret most of the spiritual disciplines I'm not doing.

Do I see a value in doing it? Yes, I feel certain that it would draw anybody closer to God. I believe expressing your thoughts in a written (or artistic) format is powerful. It can bring healing, the joy of creative expression, or deep connection with God. I think we sometimes need to empty ourselves to be prepared for what is waiting to be poured in.

We all should be challenged to look at new or additional ways to increase our faith and trust. Maybe we should allow ourselves to be stretched to try it, but with no judgment that it plays into our quality of faith. I believe journaling should only be done with a willing heart and by your own choice, through encouragement, but not based on anybody's expectations. Some people will make the decision easily because they want to try new things. Maybe they kept a diary as a child, or perhaps they embrace the idea that this could be a great faith-strengthening activity.

If you have been taught about this as one of the spiritual disciplines or feel nudged by this chapter, then I want to encourage you to try it. I want you to want to try it, and not feel obligated to by anybody. Sure, good can come by doing something out of obligation, but pure joy and love for doing it will only come when it is done with a free and open heart. Remember, God gave us free will with the hope we would choose to draw near to Him. I believe God will meet you if you journal and you may bond and connect more than any other approach you've taken. God will also meet you just as intimately if you never pick up paper or pen.

Let's look at some of the options if you want to try this. One idea that will always keep your heart close to God is to list what you are grateful for. Some things may duplicate from one day to the next, while others are new. Continually searching for the positive things and specifically naming each one while thanking God for them is a great way to start developing a journaling habit. This is often called a gratitude journal.

Reading Scripture is another wonderful source to inspire your journaling if you don't know what to write about. It can provide a simple beginning, while allowing room to grow and expand as this becomes a part of your spiritual life. If you list the Bible reference and then jot a few lines about how it impacted you, you've journaled. Our church leadership has been using the SOAP method, in which we are encouraged to reference the Scripture, note the observation of what it means, apply it to our own life and then add our prayer. Scripture + Observation + Application + Prayer = SOAP.

I have to be honest with you. I first used a phrase here more along the lines of, "At the church I attend, we have been using the SOAP method . . . " but then I realized I would have to admit once again, I am still not journaling. There is no we. They use the SOAP method, and I do enjoy hearing from the others who take this approach. I have lofty dreams to try the SOAP method more than the two times I've attempted it so far. Still, I believe this is a magnificent option and would encourage you to consider trying this. I've heard great things!

You can find numerous guided journals available for purchase. Some may guide you through a topic or book of the Bible with daily prompts, while others follow a theme like joy.

You could opt to jot down your prayers. This can be quite affirming to go back and review those and update them with answers. If you're praying for someone going through a difficult situation, it can be particularly encouraging to share the prayers with them, especially as they are answered along the way.

We've established that the decision to try journaling is yours and nobody is allowed to criticize you for not doing it, but they also don't get to tell you how it should be done. This is a deeply personal activity. If you're anything like me, if you don't feel capable or fulfilled, then you aren't likely to continue.

God Waits

If you are still searching for that style or method that resonates with you, I've got a few more ideas for you. A calendar or appointment book is one of the less daunting options and a great place to begin. You have a space for each day, but it's not as if you're staring at a giant blank page. Begin with one or two sentences in each square. Remember, what you say is up to you. Whether you are always on the go, or if you live by a set schedule, you might enjoy a travel-sized one that you can jot a note into while you are in between tasks or meetings. Consider making it a date with a small piece of chocolate or your favorite beverage to make it special. Do whatever it takes to help you enjoy the process until you decide if it's one for you to continue.

You have the option of using technology. Don't feel like it must be handwritten. You may prefer to use an electronic version and that's just as acceptable. Remember, there are no rules to follow here! If you have a good friend joining you in this, you could try a write-and-respond style of online communication for journaling. If you each create your daily or weekly entries and then send them to the other, you can respond by affirming what they wrote, encouraging them, or praying for the other and then send them back.

I don't fancy myself an artist, but I have finally accepted the description from others and will now go so far as to refer to myself as creative. While I don't have any natural talent for drawing or painting, I did think it would be a grand adventure to take on Bible journaling. If you are not familiar with this concept, this is where you will draw, paint or color pictures or words right in your Bible as you read and connect with Scripture. Some of the examples I've seen are breathtaking. They will illustrate the pages with full-color sketches of flowers or ivy trailing along the margins. The handwriting will loop and curve, taking on a life of its own. Some will even use watercolors to paint a landscape or a person from the verses.

I never had the courage to attempt it and sold the Bible I purchased for this. I think you could use the word breathtaking to describe my attempt if I had done so. My "art" would have taken away your breath, but not in a positive way! I can laugh at that and stick with the ways I am creative. I must face it, I'm such a perfectionist, I can't even bring myself to highlight or make notes in my Bible for fear of it not being done perfectly. However, I am sharing this journal idea with you because I believe it can be an amazing and less intimidating way to start for some of you.

I have always been drawn to photos, words, and especially to word graphics that are in a spectacular font or created as little pieces of art. I am a photographer at heart so I can hear full stories in my mind when looking at photos. If you are fascinated with this as well, you may want to try collage as a journaling technique. Grab one of those great big blank books and a few supplies and you are on your way to pouring your thoughts out, creating a beautiful keepsake while you're at it. Try an online photo program and add one thought using the caption feature.

This reminds me of one other very important concept within the "no rules" rule. Napkins, or index cards can be your journal. A discounted notebook or a leather-bound journal. There is no minimum or maximum cost because there is no right or wrong way to journal. You may want to consider if this is a process to release your thoughts or if you are going to want to capture them to review later. If you want to keep them, you may not want to use the napkin idea. Remember, this child of God doesn't really journal like most people would define it, but I think that my blog and this book are forms of journaling. I'm okay with that. So is God.

I refuse to count the number of beautiful journals that I aspired to use to fulfill my unspoken commitment to be a better Christian. While their pages remain empty, they have filled a purpose by reminding me that I do not have to use them to deepen my relationship with God. They are one of many options that could help me, and maybe you will find journaling helpful to you.

I have forgiven myself for not being diligent at journaling. If you need to, please consider offering yourself that same grace. God does.

I want to encourage you to try it once when you're ready. We all need to be stretched to try something we are unfamiliar with. How else will we know if it is something new to add to our practice of living a full life, while we also make intentional choices to seek God regularly? While I don't believe there are rules, owning a box full of blank pages doesn't make any of us journal-keepers, it only makes us keepers of journals.

Section Four

Lessons Learned and Learning

Who I Really Am

God, you waited as I learned some of the most important things I ever needed to know. You waited for me to accept who I am, the unique person you designed me to be.

Most of all, you waited for me to figure out how to love and be loved. Everything fell into place when my focus changed to You. I was a slow learner, and I'm still learning. I hope I never stop growing and learning again.

Thank you for waiting—and continuing to wait for the rest of my life. Your light makes me complete.

Chapter 16
Trust Issues

SURRENDER. TRUST. OBEDIENCE. Three words that can stand alone yet are far more powerful when partnered together. We are all familiar with these words, and it is not that uncommon for them to elicit a response of resistance, fear, disappointment, or outright rebellion.

Many Christians struggle as commitment ebbs and flows. I suspect it would be difficult to name one person who hasn't walked through times of surrender, trust, and obedience, only to take it all back. Then the cycle begins with the step of surrender again. This is part of a life that is being transformed. It is not a one-time decision. You can't punch your ticket once and sit back to wait until you arrive at your destination. To prevent weariness and disappointment, we need to change our expectation that we will only do this once. Instead, we must choose to persevere and seek to grow in our relationship with God.

Surrendering to God means choosing to seek God's will for our lives and putting our desires aside. When we surrender our lives to God, we are acknowledging that He is the higher power. We choose to willingly sacrifice our plans so we can live out the calling He gives us: to love God and to love others. We may not know exactly what that will look like, but we know He is in control of all situations. When I am living surrendered, I find a peace that is difficult to explain. It provides a place of rest, knowing He's the one making the plans and working out the details. I only need to be preparing my heart to say, "Yes" when He directs.

Trusting God looks different from surrendering. We may be willing to live a life for God, always looking for His guidance and plans, giving up our own. But to trust God means we choose to continue in surrender regardless of the outcome. Some definitions use the phrase, "To place confidence in." This denotes action. We must actively choose to trust God as the ultimate one we can fully trust. Putting trust in any fallen human brings a significant risk of unintentional disappointment.

I think trust may be the most difficult of these for most of us. It's tied so closely to our accomplishments. We may feel confident with the job we secured, the house we can pay for, or our health that we work diligently to maintain. If we trust God, we are choosing to be content if those disappear. We are also saying we trust God to be the same loving God as always, regardless of our circumstances or actions. It is our trust that allows us to view a lost job as an open door to a new chapter. That same trust lets us believe a financial hit resulting in having to relocate is simply a new plan from God. It's our trust in Him that allows us to face a health crisis asking God to bring the strength we need to survive but having peace if we don't.

Quite often, what I would call a hiccup in life is a moment when we get to evaluate ourselves and check on our level of surrender and trust. If we need to reset things, then let's get to it. We can learn from those hiccups and return to a life of surrender and trust.

For me, it has been difficult to trust other people because I've lived so long with the sense of being on my own when life gets tough. There were times I had expectations people would help, and they didn't. To reduce the risk of more perceived rejection, I stopped asking for help from people, or from God. I was wrong to think God would fail me or reject me. When I choose to trust God, I experience a great degree of comfort that comes from His strength.

Obedience is a tricky one based on my background and my recurring doubts about the genuineness of my faith. I used to believe if we loved God, we would have a natural response to surrender, trust and obey. I now think it doesn't come to us so easily and our willingness to live this out does not correlate to loving Him or not. I know we have a tendency to ride this rollercoaster throughout our faith journey, but I don't think our love changes. I have wrestled with the word obedience out of fear. I was afraid I could obey and choose to do the right thing without proper motives. I assumed this rendered it useless and artificial. I had lived that life growing up, simply doing what I knew God wanted, but without any connection as to why. I was afraid of going through meaningless motions again. I guess you could say I became hypervigilant watching for actions without God included in them.

I once heard it said the difference is in the why. Obedience because we believe we must is more about compliance. While that is technically a part of obedience, it doesn't bring the relationship aspect into account. When we are walking with God, choosing obedience is an act of love and worship. It can come from the heart or the mind, but it is not an item on our checklist of faith. Instead, I believe obedience is our response to God's love. It's our way of loving Him back. I used to struggle with the concept of loving God, but remember, the Bible tells us to love the Lord our God with all our heart, soul, mind, and strength.

Trust Issues

I now believe my struggle with obedience came from two incorrect ways of thinking. I didn't accept that true obedience could come from my mind only. I kept trying to equate obedience with feelings, but I didn't have any. This resulted in the fear that I was acting only out of routine, and not love. Because we know love and obedience stem from both heart and mind, I could finally accept that my obedience is genuine, even if it is sometimes fleeting.

I have always had a creative thread running through me, but lacked the confidence to believe it or pursue it. As far back as I can remember, I loved photography and often had a camera in my hands. I wrote a lot of creative short stories and even dabbled in poetry. I built trains and other models with my dad, and painted ceramics with my mom. I've been told I used to put on remarkable puppet shows, usually to an audience of our family canines.

While the medium would change, creativity was a constant throughout my life. I also had an entrepreneurial tendency, starting my first business around age eight. I never developed confidence, so I felt unprepared for what God seemed to be calling me to. I am grateful I was able to recognize His leading, even if I doubted my abilities to meet His request.

The Beginning Concept:
"You Want Me To Do What?"

In August 2011, I was blindsided by God while attending the GLS. Now, to be honest, I really should have seen it coming, as it seems this is a favorite venue for Him to reveal things to me each year, usually significant things. This time He challenged me to surrender, trust, and obey in a completely unexpected and new way I couldn't have anticipated and wasn't ready for.

While attending, my mind couldn't stop thinking about what amazing things being creative does for us. It had been a personally turbulent year with the church situation, and I found the act of being creative provided peace and comfort. I also claimed the statement others had been making to me, "I AM creative." I wanted to do something to help people, and I instantly knew it would be centered around creating art. An interesting idea, since I'm not a trained artist and do not have any natural talent. I simply enjoy being artistic and am wired to think along creative lines.

God is our Creator, and we are made in His image. This means we are also creative beings. The entire two-day event had the quality of a beautifully woven tapestry around entrepreneurship and creativity. By the end of the conference, I knew I was being led to open a place where people could experience this freedom, especially those who didn't think they had it in them. At a minimum, I wanted to help others connect with the kid inside them, while also relieving some of life's stress and anxiety. The big dream was to help them discover, or rediscover, the depth of God's love and hope through art and the healing balm it can provide.

My grandest visions included selling art to fund additional ways to help change lives. I was thinking along the lines of providing small backpacks of art supplies to kids after a natural disaster, abuse, or fire. I wanted them to have something they could call their own that would also allow them to process some of the trauma and begin healing. I hoped to work with victims recovering from sex crimes or sex trafficking, using art to bring them through recovery. I was excited about providing art supplies to a friend's church in Uganda where they had an incredible number of kids in the community.

The Delay and The Leap of Faith:
"Okay, Okay . . . I'll Do It"

Did you catch the date? 2011. It took me over three years to step out in faith. I never doubted the idea; I doubted that it should be me. Sound familiar? It's biblical.

It was evident that God had orchestrated this entire thing while He waited patiently for me to get it together and act. I found a location close to home with a landlord who had a heart for God that showed up when it came time to talk about lease costs and renovations. The view was spectacular. You could see a wall of trees across the street. I tried to deny this calling; it wasn't logical for me to do this. I couldn't deny God's nudging as I found myself surrounded by speakers, songs, and books, all pointing to stepping out. How could I ignore a book titled *Action Trumps Everything*? Several pastors around me preached sermons based on 2 Kings 3, reminding their listeners to dig ditches to see how God would fill them up. Songs like "Do Something" were playing on the radio, always reminding me to take action. Many other examples were telling me to just take one step. There was a definite theme to step out and trust God, which I could no longer deny.

I had accepted the surrender part because I didn't expect it to become necessary to move into trust, much less obedience. With such an overwhelming consistency surrounding me, I did move into trust, and out of it, and back and forth several times during the three years before I stepped out in obedience. We technically had no funds to do this, my biggest excuse, and yet, we opened our doors in November 2014.

**The Hope and The Vision:
"God, Do Your Thing."**

Every task was completed on schedule. We had a few friends rally around to help paint and move furniture in, but mostly we had God clearing the path and we had a lot of pizza—a LOT of pizza—while we worked toward our grand opening. I continued to question if this would be a success, as most would view it. Most people around me didn't understand why I would do this. I was not prone to market myself or my work. I have always been more of a background support person. I knew God was in control of this and accepted that it might provide financial security, or it might break us. It could possibly impact one life or hundreds. I understood that it may have only been a test of my faith to see if I was willing to trust God and step out in obedience when it didn't make sense to take such risks.

"Here we go God," was my prayerful invitation asking Him to be in control. In November 2014, I prayed, "The doors are open. The supplies are waiting. God, this is your place. It's up to you to bring the people whose lives you want to touch. Show me who to love and encourage."

**The Lesson Learned:
"God, You DID Your Thing."**

We kept our doors open for almost four years before I felt God's purpose had been completed and I knew we could close them. We never became a huge financial success, but I saw lives impacted because of our little creative studio space. We walked through depression with people. One client processed through a divorce as she painted and talked it out with her friends. I saw faith deepened, I saw emotional healing, I saw people connect to their creative abilities, and I saw stress melt away. I saw a dependence on God that I didn't know I had in me. It was a beautiful season I thank God for.

Surrender, trust, and obedience may sound scary or even demanding. If we look at these from the Father's viewpoint, I think it might change our perspective. I firmly believe He has our best interests at heart in every moment of our lives. He knows what is best for us and wants us to experience all He can provide. He wants us to feel joy, love, and peace while living the fullest life possible. While He gave us the ability to make our own decisions, I think He desires a life submitted to Him because He understands the beauty it will bring to us.

Trust Issues

As difficult as it can be for me sometimes to live surrendered, I never doubt that it would be the wise thing to do. It may not be that our desires are bad or would cause any harm; there could be absolutely nothing wrong with them. He alone knows what He desires for us, something we are incapable of imagining. He knows that if we trust Him and surrender our will to His, we will walk in a deeper relationship with Him. He can lavish His love on us while we simply delight in His presence. It's not that we will have an easier life, but we will have a purposeful, loved, and rewarding life by dwelling with Him.

When we think back to the times in our childhood when we disobeyed a parent or teacher, it is likely there were consequences to that even after our apology. It might have been a reprimand or punishment, like a lost allowance or privileges. The most difficult part was the expression of disappointment we saw on the face of the adult we disobeyed. We understood there was hurt there; forgiveness was coming, but we first recognized the hurt. While I think we hurt God with our disobedience, I don't know if we would see it on His face if He were visible to us now. He is more delighted by the apology and honesty than He is upset with the act of disobedience. Love is the most important thing to remember. He loves us as nobody else can.

I often think I'm doing a good job with my life and believe I am in control of things. At least until I'm not. To a certain extent, I think we are all naturally inclined toward control. I think we innately function better when there is structure or rhythm to our days. Not necessarily a schedule, but we have some things we can expect from any given day, or certainly from week to week.

I am writing this chapter while under a state-wide quarantine request due to an international virus. People are becoming stressed, depressed, lonely, exhausted, worried, and concerned as they watch incomes suffer, choices being eliminated, schedules becoming obliterated, and friends getting ill or dying. They are even more frustrated when they are confined to their homes and do not see the risks affecting their specific communities.

Dr. Henry Cloud is a well-known psychologist, leadership expert, and *New York Times* bestseller. He began doing some live podcasts during this international stay-at-home order to help people navigate the emotional toll. In one of my favorite episodes, he referred to the need to grieve the loss of control. That resonated with me. I had great expectations of what I would accomplish while ordered to stay home, but I found myself emotionally paralyzed for the first couple of months without understanding why. I'm thankful for his online show and those wise words. Because of his guidance, I was able to grieve the loss of control, focus on what I could control, see how I could help others, and I almost came to enjoy the quarantine time. Almost.

I spent the first two months of this pandemic concerned for my health and downright fearful of getting sick or dying. It took me much longer to realize it wasn't a fear issue, but a lack of surrender and trust. I trusted God with most areas of my life, like my finances, my marriage, my future, my housing, etc., but I was not trusting Him with my health. I once again had to surrender my desires to His plan. My need to take control had to be set aside so I could ask Him to take the lead. It was necessary to trust that even if I got sick, God was the same God, and I would either get through it or not. Once this lack of trust was revealed to me, I was able to pray and return to trusting Him with my health. I came to that place after a couple of weeks, and I was amazed to see all of my fear dissipate immediately.

It's so wonderful to know we can approach God repeatedly after we slide back into living for our desires or when we stop trusting Him. He is always waiting for us and will never force us to relinquish the reins. He will not criticize or judge us for trying to take over. He created us and fully understands our nature to be in charge, so it doesn't surprise Him when we try.

I picture myself standing on the banks of a slow-moving river or a lake. It's a warm day, and the sun is beginning to roast my shoulders into a light shade of pink as the sweat starts to bead across my forehead. The sun's rays are glistening on the water's surface, reflecting the cloudless blue sky. I'm ready to take a step from where I've been comfortable all day, and splash into the invigorating, yet refreshing water.

There are two choices available. The first option that comes to mind is to wade out slowly, which always unnerves me a bit. Will I step on a rock that gives out from under me and twist my ankle? Will I miss the big step where it drops into deeper water and plunge in over my head unexpectedly?

As I look up, I realize I'm standing underneath the wide, leafy canopy of a gigantic tree with sturdy branches. On one of those branches is a thick rope with several knots tied off about three feet apart from each other, beginning at the bottom. It's a rope swing that can take me out over the deeper part of the water, where I can let go and drop in with a splash.

As I climb up onto the rope, I'm filled with the excitement of what is before me. I've made my decision, and I'm going all in. I'm reminded of how confident I feel when I decide to surrender to God. My intention is to swing back and forth a few times until I reach that exact place on the arc upwards where releasing my grip drops me into the moment I've been waiting for.

But then I doubt my decision as I recall how safe I felt standing on the ground below. I am now fearful of plunging in. As I reconsider my choice, the momentum slows. Eventually, my lack of surrender leaves me suspended and exhausted. I'm not really in control, and I didn't surrender. In trying to pursue my desires instead of God's, I'm stuck. Again.

Fortunately, this swing has knots continuing up the rope, allowing me to climb safely to the branch and climb down the tree to where I'd been. I believe each time we seek to surrender, we get a little closer to taking that plunge. As we grow closer to God, I think we become so excited to splash into life with Him. We chicken out less often, we hold on a little looser, and we improve as we grow. How can we not? Maybe next time, we will let go enthusiastically and embrace the reward and joy of it.

Life is better when we live in that beautiful place of surrender, trust, and obedience. We need to continue to remind ourselves of that, so we return more quickly the next time we venture out on our own.

As I'm reviewing this chapter and making some updates, I find the timing to be powerful. I didn't want to edit this section of the book because I wasn't feeling like I was living surrendered. My prayer life wasn't strong, and due to the pandemic, I hadn't been attending church much. All of this combined, left me feeling like a hypocrite. I waited more than six months to begin. When I finally started to edit, I received a medical diagnosis that sent me to an oncologist. As I'm walking through new doctor appointments and awaiting a surgery date, I found this chapter in front of me. The first day felt like my own writing was taunting me. Through my now-steady stream of prayers, God led me to my own words, and I found comfort in them. Even though I didn't realize it, and would have denied it if anybody asked me, I found peace in discovering I was living in surrender, trust, and obedience. I'm here to tell you, these are beautiful. Please consider taking these steps.

Chapter 17

I WANT TO GO TO CHURCH

ONCE WE WILLINGLY ACCEPT AND CHOOSE to receive God's love for us, we naturally begin to change into people who love God. This will manifest itself in our thoughts, actions, heart's desires, and our attitudes. I used to dread the thought of Sunday coming when I would force myself to go to church. While this was partially due to my doubt about loving God, most of the dread stemmed from the turmoil at the church I was attending. Nothing about my faith could have changed this. While my situation was somewhat unique, it wasn't isolated. When we begin to feel this way about church attendance, we should be careful and search honestly for God's guidance. There are so many reasons we may not want to go to Sunday services. I certainly understand the value of being at church, but I'm not ever going to tell someone they must go.

What I will say is we need to be super cautious with these decisions. There have been times when I wanted to be with my husband and go for a drive on Sunday. Sometimes I feel that the extra rest is essential to restore my body's functionality and wellness from a busy week. I allow myself the grace to skip out every so often if the thought of going leans toward an obligation. Not all the time. Sometimes we need to own that the root of our excuses is a selfish desire to spend time how we want to instead of being with His church. That's between us and God, but I think we know better.

There will never be a perfect church, not even one that meets our expectations and fits our preferences. They are all filled with, and led by, people. Imperfect people. We are all imperfect people. We might be the reason somebody else doesn't want to go to church. Ouch, right? This is why it's crucial to evaluate our thoughts about it. We should pray and ask God to reveal to us what is affecting our desire to worship Him at church. If we struggle with the politics of a church, remember that church is a biblical concept. Don't throw out the idea of organized religion simply because you don't align with the leadership at your church. Seek out what the differences are. Find out why you feel conflicted. If they are not leading biblically, you may need to find another church to call home. If it's leadership qualities, or lack of them, you'll need to decide what is right for you. If it hinders your spiritual walk, you may need to consider leaving. Remember, no leadership is going to meet your expectations fully. Choose carefully. Sometimes it may be more important to remain in a church family you know than to seek a new one. However, God may also be leading you to a new home for a reason.

The truth is, every one of us belongs in any church congregation because we are one family of God's kids. Some leaders will suggest you might be your own problem if you have difficulties at one church after another. I would disagree based on my own experiences. I've noticed you usually hear this from pastors when church attendance is declining. It makes for a good deflection of something bigger that may be going on, as they try to maintain their attendance numbers. If you are unable to focus on God, to honor and love Him, to serve Him and your church family because of conflicts, then it may well be worth moving on.

If you find yourself discontent at multiple congregations, then maybe the issue is more likely to be on your shoulders after all. You are the only common denominator in what's not letting you connect. It may also be God's voice calling you to another place. Be sure to prayerfully consider everything before you choose to step out or stay.

In our situation, we were being spiritually damaged. While I wanted to foster growth and hope in the people I served, I was barely functioning on a quickly draining tank by the end of my job. It had become a toxic environment for us, hindering our spiritual growth. What heart that remained in me, that wasn't destroyed by bitterness, was now barricaded to protect the broken pieces. I felt empty, unloving, burned out, and used up. I knew God had wired me differently from the leadership there. I was exhausted from trying to speak up with what I knew God was calling me to say. I knew too much from the inside perspective and it was time to be a part of a place where I could love God and rebuild trust for church.

By the time we left, I was traumatized and wounded, while my husband was bitter and angry. In addition to losing my job, we were dealing with a variety of significant life events. We had several large emergency repair expenses equal to about 70% of my recently lost annual income. We were feeling uncertain about the stability of my husband's job as rumors of out-of-state relocation or downsizing grew louder. We had both personal and extended family health concerns. Our dog was critically ill, and we'd been misinformed that he was dying.

We didn't make the decision to leave that congregation based on the change of job status. The decision was in process for years, one step at a time. When my job ended, we were being released to act. Looking back, I can tell you exactly when we decided that it wasn't where we were supposed to be now.

We made the decision the first time we realized this was no longer the church that drew us to God. We made it when leadership did not transition well. We made it when we realized healthy places with a small staff don't go through over fifty staff changes in fifteen years. We made it based upon years of disappointment in what we knew and saw there. We made it each time volunteers or staff weren't thanked for serving sacrificially, even when they eventually broke from exhaustion or frustration. We made it when leadership would plan and talk, but rarely act. We made it when there wasn't a single leader or co-worker who said anything to me upon losing my job, other than the three I would have called friends. We made it when nobody checked on us while we were absent for several months due to illnesses and resulting sleep-deprivation. We made it when we realized we were not a valued part of the family.

We didn't attend anywhere for over six months. We didn't want to; we were just beginning to heal. There was a beautiful song that played on the radio often, as they do when new. I enjoyed the beat and would belt out the opening line and chorus because they were fun, but I had not listened to the lyrics closely. I remember exactly where I was when I first heard the song "Church" by Cochren & Co. I was making a left turn to take the on-ramp to I-205 northbound in Portland, OR from NE Killingsworth Avenue. That first time, the only words I heard were the ones I was singing as loud as possible, as I vowed I would never go back to church either.

One day, I finally paid attention to the full song. When I did, I had to pull off the road, so I didn't lose my focus on driving. It was the first time I understood that what I had been missing was the church I knew as a child. It was the first time I realized I wanted to go to church again, the whole point of the song. God used the lyrics to remind me of the best parts of church I hadn't experienced. He was opening my heart to the idea of finding a new church home and was inviting me to experience the place He knew was waiting for me; a place where we would be safe and loved while we healed. I wish I could include the lyrics here, but I can't legally. Let me encourage you to step away for a moment and listen to the song now.

The lyrics took me back to the church of my childhood, to the place my faith was instilled in me by my family, and my church family, who knew and loved me. It took me to memories of people I knew long ago and loved. It took me back to who I was when things were simpler and purer, a time and place so different it seemed like another world. It showed me what had been missing during the most recent twenty years. I longed for a place that felt like home with people I could depend on.

I didn't expect we would step into a church building for years after our last experience, but I also feared we would never return if we spent too much time away. It's easy to get comfortable in the routine of skipping church. I was afraid we were too saddened, tired, and frustrated to want to ever go through the church experience again. We started visiting a new church and believed it could eventually become a version of home, but we were afraid to commit to that possibility. I had accepted the idea of keeping one toe in church with a visit every few weeks and where nobody knew my name. It felt obedient while also non-threatening. It was safe. I was hidden. That didn't last long.

After only three visits in five months, we ruled out all other churches of interest and this was the chosen one. We attended weekly and managed to stay mostly below the radar for about six months. While it was nice to attend church without all the expectations that come with being on staff, it was difficult and awkward to be unknown. We were strangers in a foreign land after having spent two decades in a place where we knew so much and were known by most. In spiritual battle, Satan loves to convince me I don't matter, I'm not seen, or I'm not relevant. If I think I don't belong, I will isolate quickly and that's a steep, fast, slippery slope away from all God has led me to.

It was difficult to be unknown and I had to fight the desire to run. About four months in, I found myself wanting to share some sermon feedback and sent an email to Dave, the lead pastor, and his wife, Kim. This was bad timing on my part if I wanted to stay under the radar because it was only a week before a two-day leadership event being hosted at the building, the Global Leadership Summit. Part of his response was, "I'd love to catch up with you sometime, so please introduce yourself to me at the GLS."

Part of me was looking forward to connecting with new people, but I was simultaneously terrified. I hadn't been the new person anywhere in decades, and all of my insecurities came flooding back. "I won't matter to anybody" was followed up with, "You'll always be an outsider here." In those rare moments of confidence, I would throw in, "Once they know who I am and what my skills are, they'll want me to serve and I'm not ready for that."

As with any big event, there are nametags involved. I was thankful for lanyards and not sticky nametags as I diligently turned my name badge over every time he was within sight. I did this for two days! On the second day he sent the church secretary to find me, as she and I had inadvertently met previously. My cover was blown.

It was a slow process, but people started to wave at me in the lobby before church as I walked by, still trying to keep my head ducked low. Then I started to hear my name called out and a few people hugged me. I attended a women's Bunco party that took me beyond my comfort zone or interest level, just to help me become comfortable with my new church family. It's amazing what you can survive when you're obeying God! It turned out to be the launch for a couple of friendships. Finally, there were a few people who knew my name.

This church has an admirable commitment to developing leaders, something that I am passionate about. I'll never forget the time I walked into one of the leadership simulcast events and Chris, the woman at the sign-in table looked up and called me by my name. I was certain she was one person who would absolutely not know who I was. I was feeling very alone and invisible that night before arriving, and God met my empty heart through this wonderful lady who didn't know her two words, "Hi Lois," would have such a profound impact.

So yeah, I'm at a new church where I am mostly unknown after twenty years in one place. That's tough. You may be somewhere new or feel invisible. I get it. It's hard for people like us, but keep your head up, persevere in doing what you know to do, and keep showing up, because you know what? A few people now call me by name when I walk in. There is hope. You belong.

Do you remember me telling you how I would lose an entire weekend to the dread of Sunday morning coming because it meant going to church? After I settled into this new church, I developed a weekly wash of emotions and sadness that poured over me. This time, it was Sunday afternoon, after church was over. I was pained to know I had to wait seven days to see these people again, to sing praises with them, or to join in communion together. I knew I could listen to the sermons online and I would do that each week to continue the growth that began on Sundays. I was learning about God, at church! I was being continually challenged to grow closer to God, to spend time in the Bible, and to really get to know Him. I was not being nagged by a list of spiritual disciplines. I was being led by godly men and women who loved God with their whole hearts and wanted that for all of us.

After my season wandering in the desert as a prodigal, I returned to God and faith in Him. At that time, I think I still had it mixed up and intertwined with church. I had faith, but it was lost in an obligation to attend church. It was buried below the checklist of spiritual disciplines and comparisons.

If I had to start over somewhere new, I wanted to preserve that shiny wonderfulness for as long as possible. I wanted them to think I had it all together. They didn't know I had doubts. They didn't know I wouldn't pray in front of others, and they certainly didn't know how broken I was.

Instead, I trusted these people. I have shared parts of my life, my questions about faith, some spiritual struggles, my "Are you sure the Bible says that?" concerns, and some deeper personal stories with a few people I've met at this church.

Looking at the lyrics again, I am grateful. God took me to a place that feels like home, filled with people I can depend on regardless of who I am or what I do. I eagerly anticipate going to church and can't get enough of God, or these people. Go find God. He will place you where you need to be. I hope you can say it with me, "I want to go to church."

Chapter 18
LETTING LOVE IN

THERE AREN'T MANY THINGS that bring me more joy than a good road trip, especially if it takes me to a new place. I will gather some basic information about the area I'm heading to, but I am delighted most by the unplanned adventures and the people and places I stumble across on my journey. The best travel guides and internet sites cannot capture the true-life experience.

The fall following my high school graduation, our family embarked on a two-month, multi-thousand-mile road trip to see the fall foliage along the East Coast. In a small town in the Midwest, the rural highway traffic came to a sudden stop and didn't budge for over an hour. When we finally inched our Jeep and trailer along enough to see what caused the significant delay, we were in awe to discover it had stopped for a parade. Yes, a parade in a tiny town closed the rural highway as if this was something as routine as daily bathing.

We embraced this spontaneous side trip and discovered Amish ice cream in that tiny town, one of my most memorable taste experiences. The flavor was more intense than I was accustomed to, and the texture was as if velvet had been melted down and stirred in. So creamy and thick, with a deep richness I thought only royalty could experience. More than thirty years later, we often reminisce about the parade, the ice cream, the people we met who loved their town, and the ducks who used a slide to enter a child's wading pool.

There is something to be said for asking a local for directions. In addition to the necessary steps and turns to make, you may hear them refer to "as the crow flies" to tell you your destination is nearby. This only works if you could go straight there, literally as a crow would fly. When you check the map, you discover that what is a short jaunt for the feathered may take a great deal of time in a car because you must follow the winding road. There are times I settle into the journey and can appreciate the discovery process. Other days I want to be a crow and arrive at my destination directly and quickly.

I feel that way about the path between my head and my heart. My head is responsible for my thoughts, but my heart is where feelings and emotions reside. There may be only inches physically between them, but that distance can seem daunting, as if nothing can bridge the two. I think life would be much easier if I could connect them directly, as the crow flies. In his book, *All In: You Are One Decision Away From a Totally Different Life*, Mark Batterson tells us, "The distance between your head and your heart is only twelve inches, but it's the difference between information and transformation. It's not enough to invite Jesus into your mind. You have to open the door to your heart of hearts. No door can remain locked. Even the door to your hidden room."

I appreciate Mark's quote as it challenges me to be vulnerable enough to open the door. I'm more comfortable with information because I feel like it's something I can control. The head and heart seem to serve individual purposes, but I frequently ache for them to work together. When one isn't functioning in a healthy balance, it creates doubt in me, which leaves me unsettled. I tend toward using my head more than my heart, or my thoughts more than my feelings. Throughout life, it seems my feelings and emotions have been sidelined with increasing frequency, leaving me too often relying on thoughts alone. Only recently have the emotions and feelings begun to return. I can appreciate their value and purpose, but this unfamiliar experience can be unsettling and intimidating.

My natural tendency embraces the thought side of things. I love to strategize, weigh options, make lists, calculate risks, analyze, and review again before making decisions to act. I leave no room in the decision-making process for emotions. In many areas of life, this has served me well, but not in my faith. When I finally take steps, I know I did it based on an informed decision, leaving no room to doubt my actions. My problem comes later when I review the choices. As I spend time reflecting, my heart cries out and asks if it was considered during the decision-making process. Usually, it was not given a voice. This is when doubt rolls in and takes over. If I can't find an emotion to support my thoughts, I begin to question my motives.

Everybody likes to talk about feelings, right? No? A partner to feelings is emotions. Oh yes, we're going to talk about feelings AND emotions at the same time. Many people use these words interchangeably, but I want to distinguish them from each other. I think of emotions as the root cause and feelings as how it manifests itself. If I feel invisible, or unwanted, at a lunch out with a large group, it may be based on the emotion of having experienced anger at being excluded at a previous event. I think all feelings are based in an emotion.

Equally important is when they are noticeably absent. We put so much stock into both and we rely on them to indicate truth. Society teaches us that if we *feel* something, then it matters. If we don't feel anything, we are called empty and uncaring. Counselors have taught us to express ourselves to others by letting them know how we *feel* about something that was said or done; what kind of emotional impact things had. In my opinion, this confirms they are God-given and considered essential.

We can shut down our emotions for many reasons, usually as a result of trauma or fear. I think the trauma from my childhood church splitting began a shutdown process I was unaware of until decades later. I relied on my thought capabilities instead. After I returned to a life of faith, this lack of emotions caused tremendous stumbling blocks. I would sit in a church service, looking at those around me, while comparing myself to what I perceived. Many would become so overwhelmed with love or gratitude toward God that they would position themselves kneeling in submission, often with tears streaming down their faces. I felt nothing.

I once attended a GLS with fellow staff from church where they showed a video of a small child, maybe five years old, covered in filth, lying in the streets. People stepped over and around her as they passed by with complete disregard. As I looked around, many of my co-workers were sobbing, some were holding their breath, and others wore a pained expression. I felt nothing.

My feelings seemed to be non-existent. I was thrown back into wondering if my heart was so dried out and old that it had turned cold, or worse. I questioned what was so wrong with me as to be this unfeeling. How could I be a Christian and not feel any anguish for this child? If I couldn't feel broken for her, could I feel anything? Would I ever feel any gratitude toward God when I sit in church services? I returned to my old doubts that plagued me while a prodigal; *is my faith real?* Because I believed the heart was what provided emotional responses and feelings, I thought I was missing something vital. I felt the need to accept the likelihood that I would continue to question the motives behind my actions and judge them for the rest of my life. Was my faith authentic or a mirrored expression of those around me? The entire time I was on staff at church, I continued to struggle with feeling like I was a lesser Christian because I didn't feel mercy or love like they did, which contributed to me feeling like a fish out of water.

I've heard people define insanity as doing the same thing repeatedly while expecting different results. I was tired of not feeling any emotional responses and living with the questions. I decided to seek guidance from some trusted sources, even some from my new church's leadership team. I had no doubt God had placed me in this time and place for a reason, surrounding me with people I never could have anticipated. I trusted Him and decided to take some uneasy new steps. I had also recently reconnected with several people who knew me from my younger days. I was surrounded by a marvelous group of people I never could have orchestrated on my own. They all played a role in helping me understand the necessity of emotions and feelings.

God began to chip away at the guards I had installed around my heart. It was a slow process, as they'd been well established over decades. They were strong and reinforced to provide a lifetime of protection. Imagine a solid wall of cement, more than a foot thick, reaching straight up into the sky as far as the eye can see. Rebar ran through it so it wouldn't crumble, and you could see a layer of spikes protruding outward, providing a warning to those who may dare to enter.

It took over a year before I saw evidence of the dismantling. These wonderful people allowed me to ask questions, sometimes repeating myself when I wasn't ready to accept their answers. I was beginning the rollercoaster ride of believing what I was being taught, and always knew deep down. This was followed by a plunge into fear and insecurity, only to scale high again when I saw the hope of His love. Then the deepest dive into the familiar abyss of doubt would return. In December 2019, something happened that provided the missing piece to connect my head and heart for the first time, allowing me to feel God's love. The original story posted on my blog, but I have updated and expanded it here.

He Loves Me, He Loves Me Not

He loves me. He loves me not. He loves me. He loves me not. It's cute when you're a little girl and you're picking white pointy petals off a daisy as you repeat these phrases aloud. The giggles and joy disappear when you grow up and the subject of the love you're questioning is God.

What does it mean to say God loves me? What does it look like? Why don't I *feel* loved? I know He loves everybody, so that doesn't make me special, does it? Why would He choose to love me?

I was visiting friends in Northern California during the Advent season. This was a time when I needed to step away from scheduled responsibilities and intentionally focus on my faith, my writing, and my future. I needed time without interruptions or distractions. I had sermons to review, books to read, blogs to write, friends to see, places to visit, conversations to have, and had a few other ideas of how I wanted to spend my time.

LETTING LOVE IN

I had asked a handful of friends to pray for me. The prayer was my invitation, "Please, God, wash over me." I also promised Him I would say yes to anything I felt was being directed by Him and would be open to what that might be. This meant I had to be willing to change my plans and embrace His instead. Ooh...sounds like I was willing to practice surrendering, doesn't it?

God didn't waste any time.

My promise was challenged the first night. I said yes, twice, when I didn't want to. Each "yes" resulted in a deep conversation that never would have happened if left up to me. Instead, those drew me to exactly where I needed to be. As I look back, they were the first two gut-wrenching and raw conversations I had about my distressed marriage. It was refreshing to be heard, receive counsel, and gain insights from outside perspectives. The stage was set, and my heart was slowly being prepared for the events coming next.

Tommy, a former youth leader, and I had spent a good deal of time talking before the trip. He had been striving to remind me that I am a daughter of the King, a sibling to Christ, and a valuable treasure. I had not yet been able to wrap my head around the way God sees me because I was so focused on my distorted thoughts of not being worthy or valuable. On this trip, I would have similar conversations with Ed and Debbie, my former youth leaders. They were gracious to host me. I told them, "You are stuck with me for life. Once a youth leader, always a youth leader, even if I'm not young anymore."

Here's the approximate chain of events leading up to the Advent event. I spent three days exploring the town, listening to K-Love on the radio non-stop. More than 85% of the songs were chiseling at the walls around my heart, often breaking me down into tears of gratitude. Incredible conversation with Ed and Debbie filled an entire evening. During the first two days, I was engaged in over ten hours of intense and difficult real-life kinds of conversations with a few different people. God continued nudging me with reminders, and several key themes were repeating everywhere. God provided some unexpected detours that I had not planned for. I was there to attend a world-class Lincoln Brewster Christmas concert and visit a few friends. I made it to the concert, but God had a change of plans that would impact everything. I had planned to attend Bayside Church with my friend Tommy on Saturday night but instead, Bridgeway Christian Church was where we were headed.

We went to the early evening service, which was an absolute delight. The music was touching and high-quality, the sermon was relatable and powerful, and all the extra pieces flowed together to bring me closer to God. It was evident God was working on my heart through the Holy Spirit, preparing me for what would come next. They had just launched their Advent Experience, a spacious room with different stations to walk through at your own pace and focus on the four themes of Advent. This was one of God's unexpected detours I mentioned, and something I'd never heard of before. I wanted to peek in before heading out, but I was starving. I struggled because I didn't want to leave without seeing it, when my own words came back to me as if I could physically hear them reminding me, "You made a promise to God to say yes." This certainly sounded like something He placed in my path, but I was so hungry. We looked at each other, nodded yes in unison, with an agreement to each other saying, "just a few minutes so we don't miss out on anything, then we'll go eat."

We intended to stop in for less than ten minutes. I wanted to soak up all I could at different churches before returning home, and perhaps it would make for a great conversation with Tommy over dinner afterward if we just swung by on our way out.

God clearly had other plans—bigger plans. Reflecting on that night, I'm reminded of the verse in Philippians 4 where God tells us He will meet our needs. He certainly fed my deeper need when I still misunderstood what my true hunger was for.

God Waits

I stopped dead in my tracks when I first saw the paintings. They were beautiful, but it wasn't the artistic skill I noticed first. It was my knees buckling and the breath leaving my body as I focused on "Made in His Image" and "Lavished." These were two pieces of art created to illustrate God's love and the first thing I saw. I remained motionless, only three steps into the room, my eyes fixated on the paintings. I was unable to bring myself to move forward.

Tommy had advanced deeper into the room, read the sign for this first section, and was sitting on the couch opposite the paintings, reading something. There was a stack of crisp white sheets of paper on the tables with the artist's descriptions, the stories behind the paintings, Bible verses, and a prayer. This first stop of the Advent stations was simply titled Love.

Tommy quickly read through the explanation behind the paintings. There were a total of three, but these two were the ones we both connected with. Knowing my struggle with believing God loved me, he excitedly came to my side. He walked me over and stood with me as I read the sign. He expressed his gratitude for the Love section, then suggested I sit down and stay there for a while. I believe his words were, "I couldn't be more delighted with this." He showed me the detailed pages, placed one in my hands, put his arm around my shoulder, and guided me to the couches that faced the paintings before leaving me alone. I am thankful for that moment.

As I sat across from these, I realized they had touched my heart and the response I was feeling was based deeply in emotions. The first painting I saw was "Lavished." A beautiful series of colors radiated out from the top left corner. The center was white and grew into a light yellow before transitioning into gold. From there, it grew more vibrant with red that swirled into the next color, a violet shade of purple. Across the bottom was a background of the perfect, rich blue sky.

Standing in front of this was a man with his head tilted back, lifting his face toward the sun. His denim shirt was billowing softly around him. His arms were stretched straight out sideways from his shoulders at ninety-degree angles, with his palms turned heavenward, in a position to both honor God and receive.

The second painting, "Made in His Image," had a patterned, deep cobalt blue background, the color of the Caribbean Ocean. The pattern reminded me of filigree and lace, perhaps like a curtain you would find in the home of royalty. In front of that were two figures. The first was a profile view, running along the right edge, top to bottom. This figure was wearing a white robe, banded in deep burgundy, and trimmed in gold. The sleeves were large, but from the top of the openings, you could see a gold crown in His outstretched hands, resting gently between His fingertips.

The second figure in this painting was a young woman, facing him, but angled slightly toward us. She was kneeling. She also wore white, but it was a dress instead of a robe. Her sleeves bore the same deep burgundy with gold trim that his robe did. Her head was bowed just about thirty degrees forward, her eyes closed. She was in the act of having the crown placed upon her head.

The topic of many, almost countless, hours of conversations with Tommy and other key people in my life centered on my inability to grasp God's love for me, the inability to *feel* God's love for me. I was growing desperate to understand why I didn't seem to have any emotions or feelings, especially when it came to love *from* God. It was one of the themes surrounding me in the music and sermons before and during the trip. Yet, here He was, meeting me where I was, without judgment. God had been preparing my heart.

God was not only speaking to me in a language I related to, creativity, but He drew me in and held me there until I could truly understand His love for me. The longer I sat there soaking it in, the closer I came to accepting that His love was specific to me. I began to believe I was the daughter of the King. Finally, I was able to *FEEL* His love, His desire to be in a relationship with me.

Something changed. The walls I had established around my heart for protection from feeling anything began to break away in large chunks. I started to feel worthy of His love simply because of who God says I am. The voice inside telling me I wasn't worthy of love was finally hushed and I quit running from God's love. My life changed that night as I sat with those paintings. "Made In His Image" portrayed a young woman, head bowed slightly, receiving a crown. I was able to see myself in her and gradually started to accept that God really loves me that much, to call me His daughter. I have a place I belong. I am truly a valuable treasure to God. By the way, so are you. I left that night able to say, "He really does love ME that much, too." It was spoken with a slow apprehension at first, but ended in a confident tone.

The words accompanying the paintings spoke boldly into my heart—the reminder that He knows everything in me and still wants me—*wow!* The thought that we can embrace God's love, accept it, and even enjoy it left me speechless. The prayer at the bottom of the sheet of paper before me sounded like it was written specifically for me in that moment, and the tears that were cresting cascaded out. This is the full text, as provided by the artists.

"LAVISHED" - Artist: Sandra Whitehead

I based this painting on 1 John 3:1 that says, "See what great love the Father has lavished on us that we should be called children of God." I wanted to depict a man fully accepting the love God has poured down upon us, basking in that love and enjoying the fullness of it. The colorful sky behind him is that love and he stands with his outstretched arms embracing all God has for him.

"MADE IN HIS IMAGE" - Artist: Kim Nieto

This image was inspired by Psalm 130, "I am fearfully and wonderfully made." When God made us, He put together a unique combination of gifts, talents, personality traits, and genetics shared with no one else. Everything placed inside of you gives us a glimpse into the image of God. When God places a crown upon our head, He does so knowing everything about us. He knows the vastness of our potential because He placed it inside of us. God desires for us to walk in the fullness of who He created us to be. We are His daughters and sons. We are heirs of the most-high God. As His children, we can walk in His callings, purposes, gifts, and authority because it is our inheritance. Not for some day, but right now, on earth as it is in Heaven. We can ask God to show us how He sees us and what He has placed inside of us. We can rise up and walk in who God says we are, and overcome the limitations put on us by mankind. He desires to show and teach us how to walk in what He has given us and called us to do. He loves us and delights in us more than we can even imagine!

PRAYER:

Jesus, thank you for demonstrating your love for me over and over again. Deepen my understanding of your love so that I would know it in my mind and feel it in my emotions. I want to receive your love in new ways this Christmas season so that I may lavishly love others. We need your love more than anything else!

My heart was filled with love, and the smile across my lips was genuine. My emotions showed up, too, and all was well with both my head and heart. Our planned stop of a few minutes had turned into over an hour, and now I could hear the hunger grumblings. After such a mountaintop experience, it was time for a late dinner at the neighborhood diner, where a huge breakfast filled the last empty space within me, my stomach, while we continued to share our stories about how the Advent experience affected us.

On Monday, Tommy was working, but I went alone to visit the Advent Experience room to see what else God may be wanting to show me. The heartfelt impact of the paintings stopped me once again. I sat with them for almost half an hour. This time it was with more appreciation and acceptance of God's love and not the shock of how He was reaching out to me through them.

As I studied them, I absolutely believed I was the woman portrayed. I believe the artist extended an invitation to her viewers to enter the painting and kneel before God. I knew I was a daughter of the King. Seeing myself in her, I kneeled beside the painting, imagining the crown being placed upon my head.

The "Lavished" painting portrayed a man standing with arms outstretched in front of absolute radiance, allowing God's love to be lavished upon him. I was able to stand with the "Lavished" painting and physically open myself up in a matching pose. I felt like I was worthy of standing there and receiving love for perhaps the first time. With the room to myself, it gave me unlimited time and the freedom to let myself relax and have the courage to physically respond without my normal fear of what others would think if they saw me. It was just God and me hanging out.

In the center of the room was a large gold throne, with a purple robe draped across the back and seat, a gold crown resting on the robe. There was a series of large cushions at its base. The sign encouraged visitors to pray, sing, or be still. I imagined God seated there and curled up at the foot of the throne and wept openly while praying aloud. I was in the presence of my Father and was not ashamed or fearful.

After living through years of struggling to understand what God's love looks like, or feels like, I can tell you we too easily lose sight of what it looks like if we are waiting for feelings to reveal it. I simply could not grasp what it meant to be loved by God. I was hung up on my need to *feel* God's love and what I wanted love to look like. If that sounds like you, please know you are not alone but don't base truth on feelings, or lack of them. Know you are loved, accept it as the truth it is. Feelings are a bonus if they come, but not a necessary requirement.

Chapter 19
ANYTHING CAN HAPPEN

MANY CHRISTIANS HAVE MOMENTS of deep trust or connection with God. Sometimes they are connected to events we attend, like conferences, camps, or seminars. We often refer to these as mountaintop experiences or spiritual highs. Things are going so well with our faith we can't imagine life ever being different. We are fully trusting God, following Him, and spending time reading the Bible. We have a full prayer life, and we feel like there is a glow about us.

From the valley below, we see the entire mountain, looming larger than life. We begin the climb, confident we can do it and anticipating the reward of reaching the top. We might lose our footing as we step across muddy patches or loose rocks, but we persevere. It's possible we lose sight of the destination or get lost before we round that last turn and reach the summit. We've experienced the climb and have respect for the slope that can easily send us catapulting down. You will never find a mountaintop without a sloped base. It doesn't take much for us to fall from this highest peak down into the valley of life.

The good news is, regardless of where we are on the mountain, we are still on the journey. Our faith is not judged to be less than others if we aren't at the peak. We may be on top of the world or down in a creek bed under a pile of scraggly fallen branches, but faith is present and active.

I have tried to live focused on the averages instead. We're not always going to be in either extreme, but the average is a pretty good place to be. I'm picturing the small grassy cove, off to the side of the trail we were on. The cool spring trickling, and the crisp breeze blowing gently across our faces. Average is a good place to be sometimes. If we can look back at where we've been, and still have a place to look toward, let's try to spend some time on our knees, learning and growing.

We know the journey of faith is just that, a journey. When we experience the high points, we should take note of them for future review. When the low points come, track those as well. They can provide great opportunities to express our gratitude. I've learned a lot of lessons, several I had to learn repeatedly. Some came from my early childhood days, and some are more recent. We never get too old to learn new things about faith. I hope a few of my "Aha!" moments will resonate with you and save you some steps on your journey.

Somewhere, I lost my perspective of God. As a child, I used to sing, and believe, the lyrics in the song, "Jesus Loves Me." I'm guessing you remember hearing, *"Jesus loves me, this I know."* I think my head always knew He loved me. As I grew into adulthood, my heart was quick to point out He loved everybody and was eager to remind me I wasn't anybody special. This belief kept my sense of God's love distanced from me for far too long, just because I couldn't feel it. The flip side of this disconnect is that it prevented me from believing I loved Him. I was blind and did not understand what it looked like to love God.

The most important piece of wisdom I gained in this area is that feelings can't be trusted as a sole indicator of reality. I was searching for feelings, thinking they were evidence of love. I blame television and movies for that. Love is usually portrayed with a great deal of drama and emotion.

When I sealed my heart off to most emotions, my brain began to think my heart was empty. We should be careful to not stop ourselves from feeling things. We also need to be sure to keep feelings in balance with what we know to be true. Like walking a tightrope stretched between two skyscrapers, it requires a delicate balance.

I was surprised by one of the life lessons I learned, and never thought I'd believe this. The Bible is amazing! I never wanted to read through it, but I've certainly had a change of heart. I no longer view the Old Testament as a history book and the New Testament as a guidebook for living a Christian life. I understand the Bible is one connected piece. While I know I'm nowhere near the top for marks on how to live a great Christian life, I felt that I knew the requirements and didn't need to spend much time in the New Testament. I mean, once you build a house do you go back and stare at the foundation?

I didn't have a desire to read the Bible until the nudges from God surrounded me and could no longer be ignored. A conversation with a friend left me feeling incompetent to discuss doctrine. Our teaching series at church was focused on learning Scripture, and how important it can be. As a congregation, we spend a week each year focused on prayer and fasting. The purpose is to look for God's guidance as church leadership makes the plans for the next year. It is important to them to be unified in God's mission as we serve within our community. I was still new at the time, so I did not submit what God had put on my heart. A few weeks later, it was revealed that the clear direction from the congregation and leadership was the same as mine; a focus on time spent reading the Bible. The church was already very intentional about this, but here it was again as part of the vision. With those all coming together at the same time, I knew it was a guided nudge from God to start reading.

This proved difficult for me because I didn't know where to start. Fortunately, I had two ministers available who were happy to guide me through this. When I asked for the best book to get me started with a habit I wasn't naturally inclined to, they both quickly responded with, "Start with 1 John." We had recently had a sermon series based in Galatians so that was an easy next book to jump to. I've always enjoyed the letters, so I added a couple of those to the list. Rick and Dave both had suggestions that were wonderful, if not increasingly challenging, as I continued. We were discussing temptation and obedience, so Romans was strongly suggested as well. Pastor Dave reminded me, "The way of growth is indeed to 'fix our eyes on Jesus' by spending time with Him in His Word and obeying Him."

It took me several months to get started, but once I did, I thoroughly enjoyed my time in 1 John, Philippians, Galatians, Ephesians, Romans, Malachi, and Mark. Next up was Acts. Someday I'll take Rick's suggestion to read through it chronologically. This could be helpful for anybody who doesn't see how the two parts of the Bible are connected. I can't believe I'm saying this, but I'm so excited to start that reading.

This new desire was not created in me because people suggested it, nor because it's considered a spiritual discipline. It had a tiny bit of connection to a Galatians sermon series at church that I found quite intriguing. Most of all, it was developing because I was starting to love God. I wanted to hear His voice and to know His word. I was ready to have a relationship with God as never before. The desire to spend time with Him was born out of love, without obligation.

Relationship is a two-way street. God had been loving me and giving to me, but I had not been returning that to Him. I had not been investing myself in this relationship. In addition to reading the Bible, I found myself spending more time in prayer. I've always been one to pray in quick moments as things pop into my mind, but I've rarely made it through more than a handful of minutes in prayer.

The first time I was invited to the staff prayer retreat, I was so worried. I had a vision of eight hours of nothing but prayer, and I knew I couldn't do that. It was surprisingly casual; we didn't have to be seated in one spot the whole time but were free to walk, stare out the window at the beach, lay down, or whatever helped us connect with God and the others. Several people chose the floor, some were on couches or the big comfy chairs that weren't in the formal circle of hard, traditional meeting-style chairs. Still others spent the entire time standing in front of the grand windows watching the ocean waves dance along the shore, or the seagulls riding the river rapids that led into the ocean. Often there would be guitar or piano music drifting in and out as the worship pastor played softly, providing an inspiring backdrop. People took turns praying aloud or reading a Bible passage. With this blend of activities, my fear of trying to focus for eight hours was removed and I never fell asleep!

I was raised knowing there wasn't a right or wrong way to pray, and I'm grateful for that foundational viewpoint. However, I did have a few Christians come along later who believed it could be done wrong and didn't hesitate to share their opinions. A few were church leaders, and one was a friend. I didn't embrace their teachings, but it did leave me feeling very insecure about praying aloud, especially if they were within earshot.

My prayer time began to develop after I realized God loved me, and I loved Him. It took a bit of time and it started out as an intentional choice. I knew I wanted to pray. I knew I needed to pray. I wanted to be a person who prayed for longer than a minute, but I refused to do it only because I was expected to. I had to put it on my daily goal list, just to remind myself to pray. I could have been embarrassed that it had to be an agenda item. Instead, I chose to be proud that I found a way to start a new process for something that was important to me.

I love my one-minute pop-up prayers as I'm driving, taking a shower, or sitting outside with the dog. I adore listening to people pray. I'm trying to learn to ask people to pray for me, with me. It's such a heartwarming time of connection with friends when we do that. I want more, though. I want to know God is familiar with my voice and will recognize it. I want to know I can instantly recognize His voice.

Hanging out with God and having a conversation is really all prayer is. You know, God who is our Father and thinks the world of us. I think He is thrilled when we spend time with Him and want to share what's going on. I really do believe prayer is that simple. There is no need for fancy words or checklists to do it correctly. Certainly, we are aware of the example in the Bible known as The Lord's Prayer, but it isn't a rule to be followed. God wants our heart and enjoys time with us.

Jesus prayed. If there was anybody out there who didn't need to, it was Jesus. But He did. He prayed a lot and I think that's a good enough reason for me to pattern my life after His. What do you think? I think it's time we all talked with God more than we used to. My heart is lighter when I talk to God about the stuff that weighs me down. My worries about the state of the world, health, finances, busy schedules: all of it becomes lighter and my heart is freer after prayer. The happy and fun things that go on in life are made a little richer and sweeter when I tell Him about it. We don't always have friends or family to share our stories with, but God never turns away when we talk. I used to be disappointed because God wasn't tangible. He's not here in a way that can hug me or look into my eyes. Since I've started praying more, I lost that need. I've discovered I really can enjoy His presence and know He's right here with me.

Wanting to attend church was another life lesson surprise. While I grew up loving church, I became ambivalent about it before leaving it completely. While I was on staff at church, and perhaps, because I was, I eventually came to hate the very idea of church. I saw it from the operational side, with its conflicts and concerns, instead of a place to honor God.

Now, having discovered a new church home, I am shocked by my own words when I say, "Yes, I believe this is something we all should incorporate into a healthy spiritual life." When we are surrounded by like-minded people who share their own struggles while challenging each other to mature in faith, we will grow closer to God while also developing a connection with people. You can't really stop it. I tried to stay on the outside, but God draws us to Him through His people. I don't want you to go to church because somebody has thrown Hebrews 10:25 at you about forsaking the assembly. I want you to go because you love God and your Christian family. I want the same thing for myself. As much as He loves hearing from us in prayer, I'm sure He smiles warmly at the whole family all there together, loving each other.

Life has always found me serving others. I'm not telling you that to get a pat on the back or receive kind emails. I'm telling you that sometimes we're naturally wired to be kind to people, and that's a good thing. If the purpose behind kindness is to show God's love to others, it takes it to a whole new level of service. I'm fortunate. The main area I'm serving in lines up with a passion of mine. I get to show support to those who society doesn't always treat with kindness. As our faith grows, we learn to love others and it comes more naturally. Sometimes we don't feel love toward people, but we can always reflect God's love outward while our faith grows. There's no better feeling than to genuinely care for people, without any benefit to yourself. I want to encourage all of you to step into this idea if you haven't already. The world is full of people that feel unimportant. One smile or direct eye contact accompanied by, "Hello," or genuine, "How are you?" can change a life.

ANYTHING CAN HAPPEN

A decision to walk through life as a Christian may come easy for some. Spending your life living out your faith likely won't be easy or carefree. It's not supposed to be. It is real life and brings all the variety and upheavals, but with the clear purpose of living for God. Life will be a combination of standing on a mountaintop or down in the valley. We may find ourselves embarking on the thrilling ride of a rollercoaster, full of anticipation, or sitting on the safe and gentle merry-go-round. There are times when an earthquake may rattle the foundation of your faith. Anything can happen when you choose this life. But that's the great thing about it, ANYTHING can happen! God's the one in control, freeing us to live life as it comes.

Trust might come and go. Love or feelings may be strong or weak. Sometimes you will want to go to church, other times it's done from obligation. Prayer? You might not always remember the last time you prayed. The same might hold true for reading the Bible. You may dive deep into all of it or have nothing to do with any of it. You might enjoy the spiritual disciplines or run from them. None of that is the point. Doubt might even swing by from time to time. I would ask us to remember that God loves us, unconditionally. God has provided a way to be His child. It's not complicated, but it does require a decision. The sooner we let go of the worldly things we battle with, like doubt and selfishness, the sooner we find peace and freedom to live in Christ.

I feel like I've only scratched the surface of lessons I've learned, but I also know I will learn and relearn these. I hope I will learn some new things as well. We're all learning as we go. Every walk will look different. Hang on to God tightly. Get to know Jesus. Listen for the Holy Spirit to guide you. You're not alone.

Chapter 20
WELL DONE

ON A DREARY AND WET JANUARY morning, with the lyrics to "Almost Home" blasting through the speakers, I sang at full volume while driving across the expansive bridge over the Columbia River. The wind buffeting my car was a small precursor to how intensely God would impact my heart soon. I had no idea the lyrics, singing about this not being my home, would be echoed in a sermon one hour later.

It was our Vision Sunday at church, which meant the focus would be on who we are collectively as Christians, and specifically what our purpose is as a church within our local community. This was my first vision-focused sermon at Eastpark, and I almost didn't go because I thought it would be full of checklists, program updates, and the proverbial pointing finger urging us to get involved. It was still too soon for me; I wasn't ready to participate and serve.

Instead, I heard one of the most impactful sermons of my life. I don't usually take more than a handful of notes, if any. This time, I grabbed the bulletin when Pastor Dave started talking and by the time he finished, I had covered the entire page with my handwriting, which had to get smaller as I ran out of space. The notes start on the left side of the page, written in a vertical column before rotating the paper and filling the right half of the page in the opposite direction. Then the sides where there were pockets of blank space were filled in, and even the circle surrounding the thumbs up sermon theme graphic in the center of the page was filled. Our sermons are available online and I have since listened to it repeatedly because it serves as a great motivator to strive for doing better.

I appreciate that he began by asking us to consider taking notes and clarified he didn't want us to write about what he was saying, but what we were hearing individually from God. As I reviewed my notes and listened to the sermon again, I found several times when what I wrote was not in the sermon at all. God was clearly speaking to my heart that day.

I want to share every word I scrawled on the bulletin; with the hope it will touch you as deeply as it did me. Instead, let me use broad strokes to show you an overview.

We know that all Christians are going to be greeted with, "I love you, Child. Welcome home." Dave went on to challenge us to live a life God wants, so we can hear, "Well done." We were reminded that God honors our choices, and some will hear, "Depart from Me, I never knew you." God doesn't force His desires for us into our lives. Instead, He waits.

He listed five things God wants from us, and some things to think about in our own lives. I'm including a handful of points and/or questions exactly as they were written in my notes. I hope these might connect with you, even without hearing the sermon.

Living Intentionally:
- Focus. Do not run aimlessly.
- Ask myself, "What do I need to not settle for status quo about?"
- Read Bible!
- Pray!
- Love!
- Trust God.
- Accept forgiveness!
- Let God be ALL I need!!!!

Having Faith:
- Value kingdom things more than earthly things.
- What is robbing me of God's blessing?
- What is God calling me to do?
- Do I trust Him and have faith to do it?

Owning Our Identity:
- We are a displaced people.
- We're not meant to fit in!! (NOTE: Song heard on the way in today, "Almost Home")
- World values are not our values.
- Is my behavior inappropriate for a child of God?
- Every decision we make should be based on who we are.

Serving Others:
- Is self at the center of my world?
- Am I a taker?
- Who am I serving?

Paying the Price:
- Am I willing to obey and be faithful to God, regardless of the cost?
- Our "fear" or "perceived shame" keeps us from freedom.
- Am I real and transparent?
- Own who we are.
- Are we hiding things out of shame?
- Bondage will destroy us.
- Trust one person to share your source of shame with.
- Do you trust God enough to share it?
- Obey my Word and I will guide you by my Spirit.

The crown is our reward. If we spend time with God, He will guide us into His waiting arms. The official vision focus for the year was, "Trust and obey My Word; I will guide you by My Spirit and you will experience freedom."

For me, trusting God and believing His forgiveness applies to me were two of my biggest battles. I kept trying to do the work myself with high expectations of success that usually ended up as failed attempts. I should have been seeking God's help while living with the acceptance that I'm a sinner trying to do my best and not beat myself up about failing. It's okay if I can't overcome something using only my own strength. I wasn't supposed to. I didn't embrace the freedom that grace gives us, but instead I chose to continue living in imprisonment. I never thought my salvation was based on my actions, but I did think I was supposed to try to be perfect.

When I quit trying to head off sin and focused on loving and pleasing God instead, everything began to fall into place. I still sin. Who doesn't? But I started to accept that this was a normal way of life for all of us and our heart is what makes the difference. We don't decide to sin intentionally with the thought that it's permissible because forgiveness is waiting for us. We get frustrated when we sin because we know it disappoints God. Once He matters to us, our hearts hurt when we hurt Him.

My questions about how to be a better Christian were answered in this one sermon. I don't need any more coaching on this. When I love someone, I want to do things for them that make them happy. Once I realized I loved God, my heart shifted into wanting to do things that would make Him proud of me. I didn't need to ask how to trust Him or how to forgive myself. I only needed to love God, which included trust and accepting forgiveness.

I was released from the pain of needing to figure everything out on my own. I want that for you, too. If you worry your salvation is in jeopardy because you're not "doing this right," stop. Just stop. If you berate yourself because you can't stop giving in to temptation in a particular area of your life, stop. If you put yourself down for not doing everything you think is expected of a Christian, stop. I ask myself, "Would God want you talking to any of His kids that way?"

One of the most helpful books I discovered on the topic of guilt and shame is Joe Beam's *Getting Past Guilt: Embracing God's Forgiveness.* He clears up the difference between guilt and shame in a book that changed my life. One of the most impactful quotes comes in Chapter Nine, where he writes about answering Satan's lies with God's truths. We all know who's behind the lies and if we're honest with ourselves, we know they are lies. When we live with a mindset of shame, we accept the lies as truth because they keep us feeling punished, which we believe is deserved. These lies also keep us from being joyful or loving. They hinder our purpose and keep us pressed down. Joe offers simple, yet profoundly effective words of wisdom when he tells us to, "Quit thinking about how bad you've been and start praising Him for how good He is." We must take the focus off ourselves and turn it back to God.

God Waits

Everything I've learned about grace has been in the second half of my life. I grew up around biblical teaching that focused heavily on guilt and repentance, with little room for the precious role of grace. Because of this, I tend to think I'm a terrible person if I wish the guy that cut me off in traffic would get a flat tire. Most of my adult life has been rooted in shame because I had exceedingly high expectations of being as near perfect as possible. I failed. I am thankful for the spiritual teachers I have had in my life who changed my perspective. I'm thankful for those who continue to remind me of grace each time I get bogged down in guilt and shame again.

You will find a list of resources at the end of this book that helped me. If you feel bad about things in your past or feel unqualified for what God has called you to do, please look at the books listed there. I have read a lot of books, but several stand out for those who struggle with the thought of forgiving themselves. As I listened to the sermon one more time, I was suddenly aware of an alternate interpretation of the Bridgeway Advent painting; the woman being crowned. Originally, I felt it was a reminder to me of who I am, the daughter of the King. Now I see it and wonder if this might also be symbolic of receiving the crown and hearing God say, "Well done."

I sat through the church service furiously taking notes, and letting the tears stream down so fast I could hardly focus on the words I'd just written. The Holy Spirit was moving that day and moving fast. My life changed direction. God had my attention, but He wasn't through talking to me yet.

I ran a quick errand and grabbed lunch before heading south toward home. I had the radio on, mostly as an attempt to distract my brain from replaying the sermon and to get my tears to stop. Instead, "With Lifted Hands" played; a song I'd not heard before. At least, not truly heard. Ryan Stevenson's voice began, "I have tasted all this world has to offer," and I was reminded for the third time that day that I don't belong here in this world.

The lyrics continued, the singer asking forgiveness for not realizing that God is all he needs. I had never thought to apologize to God for my lack of awareness. What a touching example of how to approach God. If I had been ignoring a friend, I'd be right there asking for forgiveness, and changing my ways. The idea of God being all I needed was right in front of me again, just hours after hearing it from Pastor Dave.

I was already pulled over to the side of the road by now so I could let my heart absorb every word without the distraction of driving. That's when I heard the lyric that I couldn't help but respond to. I lifted my own hands, right there in the car. This is not a natural response for me. I am very reserved, but it was the only way I could find to express the depth of my emotion. When he sang about surrender, I knew I needed to surrender everything to Him again, in that moment. Instead of surrendering my life, my thoughts, or my plans like I usually do, the lyrics were about surrendering the days in the past.

That just got personal! If I surrendered those, I'd have to let go of the guilt and shame for things I did or didn't do, words I thought, and opinions of myself. I had carried these with me for so long they had become intertwined in my identity. I thought it would be like removing a limb from my body to surrender the days in the past. I had been asking questions about shame for years and had just finished reading several books. The seed had been planted by books, watered by discussions, fertilized by a sermon, and now this song was ready to harvest a surrendered past.

With my own lifted hands, parked on the side of a busy road, in front of a restaurant, I gave up the bondage of guilt and shame.

Chapter 21
FOREVER GRATEFUL

I USED TO DESCRIBE MY LIFE AS ORDINARY, routine, boring, drab, safe, dry, and dull. I didn't believe my story mattered. This wasn't because of low self-esteem, but because I viewed it as non-eventful, and therefore, non-impactful. My story didn't fit the mold of being one worth telling. We have all heard many extraordinary stories of triumph; people who overcame obstacles and hurdles that would have stopped most of us. Trauma has touched so many people, and yet they have survived. My story doesn't make your jaw drop and you won't hear any dramatic exclamations or intakes of air as people read it.

God put people in my life who shifted my definition of what a story is. A story lies inside each of us. We have all lived through a lifetime of days that make up our stories, whatever they may look like. I believe that what is unremarkable to one person may bring hope to another.

What sounds boring to me about my story might give someone else confidence. We will never know who needs to hear our story, but I want to encourage you to share yours. Yours is a life worth talking about and celebrating.

I have been around a lot of people who not only have exciting stories, but they tell them well. People hang on every word, leaning in, eagerly waiting for the details to unfold. I can remember hearing the reactions of people and the conversations afterward. I enjoy listening to stories, but they used to leave me feeling inadequate to tell mine. I would always compare them to my life. There's a common phrase I hear that cautions us, "Don't compare their highlight reel to your behind-the-scenes story."

God frequently reminded me we are all created uniquely for a purpose. When I started to share my stories through my blog, I didn't hear the reactions. I didn't have staggering numbers of followers or comments. What did happen was people wrote to me telling me how much they connected with what I had shared. They thought they were alone in their experiences and appreciated hearing my story and perspective. So instead of the shouts and noise, I received quiet confirmation that there was someone who needed to hear what I had to say. For that reason, I chose to share my ordinary life.

Numerous times through the years, I've heard leadership speakers talk about the need to celebrate more often. They aren't just talking about the milestones like birthdays and anniversaries, or even new jobs or births. They are trying to teach us to celebrate any win we get and any progress we make. It is through celebrations that our hope is renewed, and our excitement and enthusiasm are reignited.

I started celebrating more in recent years. I was once part of a group of four friends who met regularly to encourage each other to work on our goals and projects. We adopted the name Creative Think Tank because most of the goals were centered around creative-based dreams. I will always treasure the time spent with Dana, Carmen, and Amy as we learned to hold each other accountable and cheered each other's wins. We adopted the Micro-Movement Wheel of Delight, a tool we discovered from the author SARK. It looks a bit like a casual pie chart. You list tasks around the wheel that take between five seconds and five minutes to complete, but will move you forward, toward your goal.

Celebrations are great reminders that we are making progress. They encourage us to continue the process even when it isn't easy. It is important to find friends who will celebrate with us along the journey; we all need cheerleaders.

Sometimes we celebrate things that seem odd to others, but we are the only ones that can see things from our perspective. Celebrate anyway, even if you're the only one. The day my job was eliminated, we celebrated as a family. We didn't take long because of the sick dog, but we did go out to dinner. We never shed a tear and only looked forward. We celebrated again on the first anniversary and will probably continue to do so until we forget to look at the calendar.

Why did I celebrate a year without income, a year when we should have lost our house or had to sell a car to survive, a year that brought significant change to our routine after almost eighteen years in one place? I celebrate that day because I was set free. It was a life-altering day that was the catalyst for a better life. When a new product or book releases, it's celebrated with a launch party. We now declare that day as Lois's launch day. It was the first step to becoming who God created me to be, to see the fullness of life He had waiting for me, to discover how much He loved me, to meet the people He was connecting me with, and to do what He designed me to do.

I celebrated because God overwhelmed me with His love that first year. When I was in a content mindset, not necessarily turning to Him, He waited patiently. In the few instances when fear crept in and I felt despair, I knew I could cry out to Him. It was God, the one true and constant companion and faithful guardian, who yearned to welcome me into the plans He had created specifically with me in mind and been waiting years to show me.

I knew God had put it on my heart to be a voice for Him, but I had been mistaken about who the audience was to be. I had a small picture, but He had a bigger plan. He had been whispering to me to for years, giving me permission to leave. In my naïve loyalty, I thought the people at my church were my audience and I was trying to be obedient to God's guidance.

The looks on the face of parents when their child begins to take steps is one of pure delight and joy. Can you imagine how much more excited our Father God is when we take the right steps? I can almost hear God giggling with the anticipation and excitement as He waits for us to wobble and step.

When I wrote a note to the pastor's wife, Kim, in late July 2019, she responded with an invitation for coffee. I was shocked. I wasn't used to people I didn't know reaching out to minister and care for me.

I had been working to figure out what my next steps should be regarding employment and ministry. I missed serving at church, but I also wasn't sure I had enough left in me to give. My guilty conscience was telling me it was time to volunteer. I honestly think I sought out obligations and distractions, so I had an excuse to not sort through the trauma I'd experienced. I didn't want to go through the hard stuff yet, and process emotions like grief and anger.

As we sat outside with our beverages, listening to the planes flying overhead as they departed the airport, I found myself telling her I was going to try freelance work. I was in the process of deciding what types of services to offer in my new small business. One area I was preparing to step into was providing project and administrative support to small businesses or individuals who could not afford staff.

I was excited about an idea I had, a specific style of personal accountability and coaching I wanted to offer. Excitedly, I poured out, "I want to be an accountability partner for people who can't afford life coaches but need someone to check in on their progress." Kim quietly responded, asking, "Is anybody doing that for you?" I stared back with tears in my eyes. Her next reminder put my plans on hold. Quietly, she suggested, "Be sure to work from a place of rest, rather than need to rest from work." It's something that stuck with me, and she attributed it to *Building a Discipling Culture* by Mike Breen.

This was a pivotal moment, and it came from somebody I would never have expected to step in. I want to encourage all of us to listen for the fresh voices God may be providing. I had placed expectations on people who had been a part of my life but never checked on me. Now, here was this wonderful stranger treating me like I mattered because I was a fellow child of God. She didn't know me at all, but her words were the nudge I needed to take the next right steps after ignoring my need for healing from the tumultuous years at work. She counseled me to take some time for emotional and physical restoration and encouraged me to take the time to grieve. There had been many losses throughout the years, and it was time to acknowledge the hurts and disappointments of life, draw closer to God, and most important of all, be still. With much affection and appreciation, I now refer to this as the time the pastor's wife, Kim, put me in "Time Out."

It took a few months before I finally chose to become still so I could hear God's voice. Wow, was He ready to speak! He spoke countless words of comfort, healing, love, affirmation, and even some challenges. He spoke words of anticipation and delight. He knew the future plans, to use my gifts and bring restoration. He guided so diligently when I would allow Him to, but never forcefully. He waited for me. He waited a long time for me. Because God loved me so much, He led me to what He had prepared for me and who He provided to accompany me. I never imagined it would take almost four years to be restored to my pre-employment state of mind.

Gratitude Abounds

Friendships: I have people in my life who never would have crossed my path without the church job. Well, technically, I can't know that. God can do some pretty mysterious things, but can we roll with it for now? Several people I met there continue to speak into my life, my marriage, my character, and my faith, and I into theirs. Regardless of where we attend church or what state we live in, we are family. We are friends, for life, and eternity! I would never trade them for a different path through easier circumstances. Many of us went through those tumultuous years together, and that makes for a deeper bond than average.

Faith: My faith took a hard hit while working at the church. I began the job believing my rededicated life was all I needed. I couldn't have been more wrong. I had the basics of faith, but most of the spiritual growth that brought me to where I am, came either during, or in response to, my employment experiences. I continued to question my faith at times. It took a cancer diagnosis to see my faith show up, leaving no room for uncertainty. My faith is more real than I knew. Thank you, God, for using that trial to reveal your truth.

Church: It was a tough start, being new somewhere after having been known where I was for almost twenty years. But you know what? I am fortunate to have found a church that is home, a place where I belong. It provided a refuge while I healed, while God restored me. Even though I now attend alone, I still feel at home there.

I found this church because of circumstances originating in 2007 at the GLS. I believe God had been orchestrating this all along and was preparing the way for me. I appreciate being part of a church with leadership that holds the people accountable to living the most Christlike life we can. We are challenged regularly to deepen our relationship with God, and this is what I have unknowingly craved most of my life.

Through the joy of technology, I can also listen to the sermons of several key people that encourage me to love God with all my heart, soul, mind, and strength. I am grateful for every one of those people that continue to speak into my faith, deepening my love for God.

God: I can imagine God tapping his fingers, counting the days as He waited for me to move forward into this next season. He knew how incredible it was going to be and what gifts He had waiting for me. He slowly unwraps these and presents me with His treasures regularly. I am slowly developing a relationship with God through a desire to make Him happy. I know I trust Him and love to spend time getting to know Him. I can now say I love Him, and that is an amazing place to live in.

Dreams: I have found a new church home. God has surrounded me with people I never would have met, who love me, keep me encouraged, and hold me accountable. He even paved the way to connect with many people I had lost contact with. I'm writing with the confidence that others have been trying to instill in me for years. My passion to be creative is returning as I dust off the camera and plan more road trips. You're reading my first book! After so long living without dreams, I'd say I'm pretty much "living the dream" now.

This list of blessings could be updated on a weekly basis. He even used the quarantine time during the Covid-19 pandemic to provide some unique opportunities that have propelled me forward into His plans. I keep saying, "Yes," because I now know His voice so much better. Don't get me wrong, I certainly haven't perfected listening, but it's more recognizable and I also have more people I can pass things through to help me discern it when I'm in doubt.

I want to encourage all of us to listen to God's voice and not be complacent. I dare us to say "Yes!" to God's calling and not be content when we feel nudged. Mostly, I beg us to connect with people until we find the ones who deeply love and care for us, expect nothing in return, and will speak wisdom into our lives.

I cannot comprehensively list the variety of ways God has taken care of me and shown me a future I couldn't imagine. The diverse and unique group of people He has surrounded me with come from an assortment of doctrinal backgrounds, unified by their love for God and for me. I try to thank them, and I do pray they know the difference they are making. They are restoring me to the best of who I used to be, challenging me to grow into who God made me to be. I will forever be grateful to have "Team Lois" keeping me learning and growing.

For those who know part of my story, you may have been tempted to figure out who did what, or said the words I quoted, especially as it related to my church employment years. I invite you to hear me clearly. This celebration is about what God ADDED to my life. There are a handful of friends from those days that remain a part of my essential core group. My life has become a beautiful blend of God's family. I will always celebrate those people.

I know I wouldn't be the person I am without the people who love me, encourage me, and challenge me. I'm not above begging you. I firmly believe it is critical to your life, get the right people around you. Get the people who you can cry out to when you fail. Get the people who will pray for you. Get the people who will speak God's word into your life. Get the people who love you. Get the people who value you. Get the people who remind you of your purpose when you lose sight of it. Get the people who will speak tough love and accountability. Get the people who challenge you to try new things. Get the people who are transparent. Get the people who will listen to you. Get the people who will see you. You have those people. It may be that you haven't crossed paths yet. Maybe they are different from who you thought they would be. It's also possible they are waiting for us to be that person for them.

I spent decades mostly as an island with a drawbridge I could let down for a select few. God knew I needed a community, and when I started seeking His provisions and His will, He provided.

Now I celebrate. People listen to me and call me by my name; I am seen. I have connected with people from almost 40 years ago who speak volumes of wisdom and cheer me on; I am encouraged. I am invited and included into Bible study groups; I am wanted. I have a handful of wise men and women who pray for me and offer accountability; I am mentored. I have wonderful people who have invited me into their home to visit; I am welcomed. I have people who see my desire to be more and are coaching me; I am challenged. I am living a full life, doing the things I believe God had planned for me; I am content.

Forever Grateful

Each day is a celebration because I can be sure of one thing as vividly evidenced through this journey. I am loved. I am loved beyond measure. I am loved not because of my own doing, but because I am special to The One. I still have a collection of blank journals and my Bibles are still dusty, even the one my friend Tom bought for me. God loves me regardless. I am not a "lesser" Christian, and neither are you.

Please join me in living a life of celebration as you believe you are loved and wanted, seen, and welcome. I didn't accept or believe that readily. My belief still fluctuates regularly. I know this is joyous and terrifying at the same time. So many of us have felt the opposite for so long, but maybe it's time we listen to the people trying to show us we matter. Maybe it's time we listen to God and not the hurtful words of others, or ourselves. He is whispering over us, "I love you. You are precious." Now, go celebrate that fact!

I told you I'd answer the question about my church job before this book was done. I am thankful I never felt defined by my job. It was once a calling but that changed. When my pastor told me they needed to reduce my hours due to budget cuts, he said, "It's just a job, do what you need to do." He was giving me time to process keeping the reduced position or seeking a full income elsewhere. I was stunned to hear it could be "just a job" to anybody.

None of us are defined by our jobs, what people say about us, what we tell ourselves, what our finances are like, or anything else based in this world. We are all defined by who God says we are. I promise to try to remember that if you will, too. I would not knowingly choose a path today that caused as much pain as working in the church did for me.

However, without that time, I would not have the life I have today, the people I count as family, the church I now call home, the faith I no longer question, the love I can accept unconditionally from God, or the love I now freely give to God. The life I have now is worth it. I am open to saying, "Yes!" to God's leading, and if that means working in a church again, a different one, I'm all in. If it means never working in a church again, I'm good with that. I value most of the experiences and all the friendships that came from that time. I value the discernment gained from what I saw happen. I deeply treasure the outcome and am thankful for that time because it led me to "now." So yes, I would do it all again, if I knew where I'd end up afterward. There is no price too great for the reward.

I survived church and found God.

Resources for You

REFLECTIONS ABOUT LABELS

FIND A PLACE WHERE YOU CAN BE UNDISTRACTED and quiet for a few minutes to think through something. What are some of the labels you've been living with? I hope they're positive ones, but don't be afraid to include any that come to mind first. I'll start you with a few that I created for myself, based on lies. The first ones that come to mind include: unwanted, invisible, unworthy, insignificant, ugly, prodigal, and incapable. I don't think I'll be alone in having mostly negative labels I use to identify myself as.

I want you to take a few minutes and imagine your labels. I'll leave you some space here in case you want to write any of them down.

Now let's look at some new labels together that apply to all of us. Prodigal might not, but we all have plenty of other labels to focus on.

My *Beloved* label is the crisp blue of a summer sky with thick, bold white brushstroke lettering. *Cherished* is far more elaborate with fancy script on a pastel yellow that feels like the rays of sunshine streaming through on a porch. I can't see *Forgiven* without picturing the lines and circles in the grain of wood, like that of a cross. I've always been drawn to the beauty of a gorgeous woodgrain, it's so rich and luxurious. On this label the word forgiven is written by hand on the bottom right corner, like a signature on a check signed by Jesus, paying the debt.

Like the one lost sheep that the Shepherd seeks out, my *Valuable* label is white and drawn to look like wool. It serves to remind me of how important I am to Him. Shiny silver foil is where you'll see the word *Treasured* in an old-world embossed style. My *Wanted* label looks like it came out of the old western movies with my photo on it, just below the title. *Rescued* is red and white check, like a life preserver on a ship and the lettering is stenciled in black.

There is one in the center, the color of caution tape yellow, with large block letters forming the word *Prodigal*. It means a lot because it reminds me of the dangers that wait for me if I lose my way again. It serves as a beacon to

Reflections About Labels

point me back before it's too late. My absolute favorite one is *Daughter of the King*. It is beautiful and colorful, with royal blue, white, and burgundy forming a textured background. The letters are gold, and larger than life. It fills up the entire label and will always be one I keep on top, completely unobstructed. There's even a small crown in the top right corner. I've based this off of the painting I wrote about, with the woman receiving her crown.

Somehow, I know she wasn't perfect. I know she stumbled in her walk. I know she had doubts. I know she compared herself to others and found herself coming up short. I know she didn't always read the Bible or pray like she thought she should. I know she skipped church. I also know she is the Daughter of the King and He is so overwhelmed with love for her. He takes joy in her being near Him. He could not be more delighted to have her with Him, and He feels the same way about every one of us.

Rest in those words. Ask God to show them to you. I can remember pictures better than words, so I hope by doing this exercise you'll be able to call them from your memory when you need them.

As I apply these new labels, I'm not able to see the old ones that kept me imprisoned. They are being replaced. Like our physical scars, I know they are there and can barely feel the raised edge underneath the new ones that are my true identity. They may have shaped who we are, but we are not our scars.

MUSIC AND MENTIONS

MUSIC GETS INTO THE DEPTHS OF MY BEING like no other source of input. I'm including the songs I referenced and a few others that were a part of my journey. I'd suggest discovering some of these on your own.

I often blog about songs and share the story of why they carry such a deep meaning for me. I usually include links to the videos since I can't share the detailed lyrics. It's a lot of fun and I'd love to keep you inspired and entertained, so check out the blog and bookmark me! There are so many I want to list here, but you'll find them on the blog. Have fun!

LoisFlores.com
ThatResonates.Blogspot.com

God Waits

"Church"
Cochren & Co.

"Almost Home"
MercyMe

"With Lifted Hands"
Ryan Stevenson

"When God Ran"
Phillips, Craig and Dean

"Morning Light: Songs to Awaken the Dawn"
Steve Green

"No More Pretending"
Scott Krippayne

"My Eyes Are Dry"
Keith Green

"Dive"
Steven Curtis Chapman

"I Will Follow"
Chris Tomlin

Music and Mentions

A few of the other interesting bits I mentioned:

North High's Beloved, Coach Turk Eliades
https://www.greeks-in-foreign-cockpits.com/pilots-crews/fighter-pilots/jordan-eliades/

SARK's MicroMOVEment Miracle Method
planetsark.com/Miracle

Tinikling Filipino Dance
https://youtu.be/_WLfqDMwA_o
That's a lot to type, so you can do an internet search for "2017 UCLA PCN Filipino Tinikling" on YouTube. This is a great video posted by Rick Cadiente.

PEOPLE WHO INSPIRE ME

LOOK FOR THESE PEOPLE to see who inspires me. I'm including current website information, but search for these people on your favorite podcast and social media platforms as well.

Jon Acuff
acuff.me

Bob Goff
bobgoff.com

Bayside Church
baysideonline.com

Brant Hansen
branthansen.com

Brené Brown
Brenebrown.com

Bridgeway Church
bridgeway.church

Candace Payne
candacepayne.me

Carlos Whittaker
carloswhittaker.com

Christine Caine
christinecaine.com

Daniel Fusco
danielfusco.com

Eastpark Church
eastpark.org

Erwin McManus / Mosaic Church
mosaic.org

Lance Hahn
lancehahn.com

Zoro
zorothedrummer.com

A Few Books I Found Helpful

BE SURE TO KEEP AN EYE ON MY BLOG for more books I would recommend. There are so many wonderful authors and I enjoy sharing what I discover that inspires me. I mentioned most of these but tossed in a few other current favorites.

LoisFlores.com
ThatResonates.Blogspot.com

Blessed Are the Misfits
Author: Brant Hansen

Dare to Lead
Author: Brené Brown

Getting Past Guilt: Embracing God's Forgiveness
Author: Joe Beam

Sacred Pathways: Nine Ways to Connect with God
Author: Gary Thomas
NOTE: Earlier edition is Sacred Pathways: Discover Your Soul's Path to God

So You Don't Want to Go to Church Anymore: An Unexpected Journey
Author: Wayne Jacobsen and Dave Coleman

SOAR!: 9 Proven Keys For Unlocking Your Limitless Potential
Author: Zoro

The Master's Mind: The Art of Reshaping Your Thoughts
Author: Lance Hahn

The Soul of Shame
Author: Curt Thompson

Through the Wilderness: Finding God's Presence When All Seems Lost
Author: Carol A. Brown

More About the Author

GOD WAITS IS LOIS FLORES'S DEBUT BOOK. She semi-faithfully updates her blog and contributed to *We Become a New Story: Writing from women, men and young adults healing from cancer, Knight Cancer Institute.*

Her parents teased her about talking too much, so she took to the written word at a young age. She is thankful to have several of her first creative writing pieces dating back to elementary school.

She resides in the Pacific Northwest where she feels like she doesn't fit in because she dislikes coffee, salmon, hazelnuts, and hiking. Sometimes she enjoys rainy days and believes that might make up for it, and her husband drinks enough coffee for two people.

Her furry companion shares a name with a troll and accompanies her on frequent road trip adventures, where she's always looking for the next great photo opportunity.

People matter to Lois, and she strives to encourage those she meets along the way. You can often find her by listening for her laugh.

A daily battle wages between her left and right brain, as they fight like siblings for equal time.

She considers herself a biscuits and gravy aficionado and thinks the glue that holds life together includes waffles, road trips, God, cheeseburgers, dogs, beach time, cinnamon rolls, music, resilience, friendships, and tacos! But not necessarily in that order.

LoisFlores.com

ThatResonates.Blogspot.com

With My Deepest Gratitude

IF OUR PATHS HAVE CROSSED, whether directly or indirectly, I am grateful for your influence in my life, and in my faith.

If you wondered if you might see your name here, then you are someone I dedicate this book to.

I am deeply grateful for the path God led me down to find Him, and all the people He placed alongside me.

www.ingramcontent.com/pod-product-compliance
Lightning Source LLC
Chambersburg PA
CBHW070137100426
42743CB00013B/2730